TALES FROM OUR TOWN

By Reading Writers

Edited by Miranda K. Lloyd

First published in Great Britain in 2016 by St. Marks Publishing
21 St Marks Road, Henley-on-Thames, Oxon, RG9 1LP

ISBN 978-0-9572636-5-9

Typeset in Garamond by Andy Bennett

FSC sustainable

Printed and bound in Great Britain by KnowledgePoint Limited, Wokingham, Berkshire.

FSC

Also available as an eBook

www.readingwriters.co.uk

Contents

Acknowledgements

When it was suggested that the time was ripe for another Reading Writers' anthology, I eagerly volunteered to edit it. 2016 is Reading's Year of Culture, and what better way to celebrate this beautiful town than with a collection of lovingly-written short stories, poems and non-fiction from talented local authors?

Reading Writers has taught me everything I know about creative writing. Members work together to provide a friendly and supportive atmosphere in which all writers (and editors!) can thrive. It's been a privilege to edit this collection on behalf of the group and I'd like to thank everyone who has helped make it happen.

Special thanks go to: Katy O'Hare for the wonderful cover; Juliet England, John Froy, Charles Whittaker, Rob Wickings, Josh Williams and Julia Bohanna for proofreading; Andy Bennett for typesetting; Claire Dyer and the Reading Writers' committee for giving advice and marketing support; Reading Central Library for hosting the launch; Reading Museum for being the source of inspiration for many of the pieces; KnowledgePoint for printing the book and Ben Smith for providing moral support.

Miranda K. Lloyd
Editor

ABC to Read
Assisting Berkshire Children to Read

ABC to Read is a local charity in Reading. We recruit, train and support community volunteers to provide one-to-one mentoring for primary school children who are struggling to read. We work to advance the education and self-confidence of primary school children in Berkshire by helping them to overcome reading difficulties, making reading fun and giving them a skill for life while promoting their general well-being. We're always looking for volunteers. Find out more at *www.abctoread.org.uk.*

AT HOME

The Baroness's Daughter

John Froy

Eva von Sacher-Masoch, Austrian aristocrat,
turned up in Milman Road without a car or phone,
sent her daughter to St Joseph's Convent,
charitably subsidised, just along the road –

she was trying to salvage something
after Major Faithfull, ex-MI6, mad inventor,
had thrown them out of Braziers commune,
home to neo-paganism and Woodcraft Folk.

The latchkey child went to Holy Joe's.
For years, I imagine, she trudged past,
hair up, convent uniform outrageous,
now a young member of Progress Theatre.

She learnt from the Index of Banned Books,
bought and smuggled them in past the nuns,
then ran away to London, and suddenly
As Tears Go By was Number One.

She was Jagger's girlfriend, decadence
personified, and scourged by the press.
I was still at school, but tuning in hard
to all tomorrow's parties.

When I put on my patchouli-oiled coat,
she had moved to a Soho wall,
sharing fires on a bombsite in St Anne's Court,
twenty-five heroin jacks on the NHS

from John Bell & Croyden, the chemist.
I felt her when I walked those West End streets,
heard her climb back through the songs,
that cracked gravel sound of Kurt Weil.

We played *Broken English* in the language school,
listened in awe to *Why'd Ya Do It?*
I'm so glad, Marianne, you pulled through.
I still live between the convent and Milman Road.

A Knight For Five Kings
Rob Wickings

The thunder of hooves. The sweet weight of armour binding me, cradling me. The lance, thrumming and leaping in my hand like a living thing. The moment I am most alive.

And I remember...

*

When I was five years old, the King of England loaded me into the bucket of a catapult and threatened to fire me at the walls of Newbury Castle. It was a desperate tactic from a desperate man. My father, John Fitzgerald, Marshal of the Horse, had backed King Stephen's cousin Matilda as rightful heir to the throne. His Majesty was rightly peeved at this insult from a subordinate.

The walls of Newbury Castle were solid, and the siege that Stephen undertook would be long and painful on both sides. My father, it transpired, was a very stubborn man and would not pay heed to the king's reason. Even when Stephen held a strong bargaining chip. Me.

Now, John and Stephen had a long and fractious history. These were tumultuous times, and John had not helped matters by backing and then withdrawing support for his King. The two had been indulging in a breakneck chase across England for the better part of ten years. John had lost an eye during the siege of Wherwell Abbey to hot lead dripping from the roof after Stephen set the building on fire. My father had always had a jaundiced view of the world, which the loss of half his vision did not mellow.

You might ask, then, why John would give me to Stephen

as a hostage in the first place. Not the most tactically astute move, surely? Well, things were done differently back then. It may not have seemed that way, but there were certain rules, especially when under siege.

*

Rules. As rigid and intractable as a knight's path. Straight and true and inviolable. Like my many excursions down the lanes of the joust, one with as inevitable an end. I have made my name in these places. God has willed I have a little talent. They call me reckless. William the Wild. Perhaps I am bold in the face of death. But you see, death and I have been on nodding terms for a very long time.

*

Loading a child into a catapult and threatening to lob him at Newbury Castle? Aye, I'll admit that stretches the bounds of honourable behaviour. But, as I said before, John was not a reasonable man, and we had been at this pass before. You see, some weeks previously, Stephen had set up a gibbet in full sight of the castle ramparts, and threatened to have me hanged unless John surrendered.

My father's response to this has gone into history, although I don't remember him saying it. I was quite distracted. There was a lot going on around me, what with the soldiers fussing around and the rope about my neck.

John had looked down from his tower, and dared Stephen to do it. He said, 'I have the anvils and the hammer with which to forge still better sons!'

It's a good line, but I doubt my father said it. He was a man of few words, mostly the pungent sort that a peasant would sling at a recalcitrant pig. That sort of punchy one-liner would have been beyond him. But, as the scribes say, "when the legend becomes the truth" and so on.

I return the story to the bucket of the pierrière, the wall-breaking catapult that Stephen had ordered up to firing range. Ever-thoughtful, he had placed a cushion in there for my comfort. A strange notion, but the rules of engagement bound the king to certain duties of care.

*

This moment would become the defining moment of the siege of Newbury Castle. You can probably guess how it ends, as I am here telling it to you. But it has pertinence to the issue at hand. I have misjudged you, sir. They called you young and callow. I saw your nervousness at the slips, and judged you an easy victory. Perhaps these reveries into my past have slowed my hand a fraction. For it seems you have struck me true. You have unhorsed me, sir. Our relationship enters a new stage, in which you have the upper hand.

This too is a position with which I am familiar, alas.

*

'I will smear your son over the walls of your castle like an over-ripe plum! My patience is worn thinner than your sense of honour!'

Stephen, normally pale and calm, was red-faced and shaking with rage. He could see John and his family ranged across the balcony facing the besieging force. My mother clutched at my father's arm, sobbing. My father as unmoved as the stones at which I was about to take a sudden and very close look.

11

'What do I care? Making sons is easy. I can always replace that mewling brat, and next time I'll do it right!'

Now, allow me to point out that I was not mewling. I had always been a quiet child, watchful and serious. I watched the king now. The fingers of his raised arm trembled slightly. He glanced across at me. I saw something then that I had never seen before. A look that, alas, I would come to know all too well in my future career. Sheer terror.

Stephen had backed himself into a dark corner. If he gave way to my father, the humiliation would be hard to recover from. If he did not, if he called John's bluff and lowered his arm…

Well, there are few rewards in heaven for the killer of a child.

'Hurry up, my Lord,' John roared from the safety of his castle walls. 'My dinner awaits, and I need to know if I must make a new son tonight!'

Stephen's jaw tightened. He fired a hate-filled look at his adversary. The moment was upon us. In the next five seconds, I could know how it felt, for a brief moment at least, to fly. Silence hung over the field of battle. I played with the fringed corner of the cushion on which I sat. A mottled gold damask, I recall. Strange, the things that come back to you in stressful moments.

And then Stephen looked at me again. The terror melted, replaced in an instant with utter surety.

'Step away, boys,' he said quietly to the pierrière crew. 'The minstrels will call me many things in their songs, but Stephen the Boy-killer will not be one of them.'

He dropped his arm, turned and walked away as the jeers

rose from Newbury Castle. But the set of his shoulders was not that of a defeated man. You see, my king had learned something that day about the power of mercy. That wisdom would see him peacefully retake Newbury some months later, and eventually restore him to the throne of England, to start the long process of bringing peace from anarchy.

*

Which brings us back to the here and now, sir. You, like my father, believe you have the upper hand. Certainly, you have unhorsed me. Yes, I am on my back in the dirt with your blade to my throat. And yet, our day is not yet over. I have seen that look in your eye before. It is not the look of a man on the brink of victory.

So, no, sir knight, I shall not yield. For I know of the life to come, and matters do not end here.

My name is William Marshal, sir, of Caversham. My sword will serve five monarchs.

When I was five the King Of England failed to kill me. Twice.

What on God's green earth gives you the notion that you have a chance?

A Door In The Sun

Claire Dyer

Cut a door in the sun;
with warp and weft weave the yellow in.

Dye wool indigo, sage;
make leaves into butterflies, birds.

Go barefoot in the bulrushes,
feel river water between your toes;

pick harebells, fritillaries
for our blue china vase –

there'll be earth
beneath your fingernails.

Tomorrow we'll weigh our words,
tie the ends of them together and

listen to the meadow sing.
For now, wrap me

in the near night and light
and half-light. Hold me.

After John Piper's tapestry 'Rural Reading', which is currently held in Reading Museum, and W. B. Yeats.

Caversham Park Village

John Shepherd

After all this time I can't recall what we had planned to buy in Reading that day in 1970. I will, however, never forget what we bought instead. Neither can I remember why we approached Reading via Sonning Bridge. Now it seems a very illogical route to take from Bracknell. However, in 1970 the A329(M) did not exist and the Inner Distribution Road was incomplete. I suspect that we were heading for a shop north of the railway line just off Caversham Road.

As we passed the foot of Caversham Park Village we both noticed the sign advertising new houses for sale. We lived in a pleasant modern rented two bedroom flat in the Harmans Water area of Bracknell. We were happy there and had no intention of moving. Both sets of parents had lived in rented accommodation all their married lives and it hadn't occurred to us to do anything different. However, there was no harm in looking. There were 11 houses up for sale and we got the keys to look over the show house. It was a three-bedroomed semi with a built-in garage. We loved the location, just 100 yards from the countryside but convenient for the local shops and just a short bus ride from Reading town centre. The garden was small enough to require little work but large enough for kids to play in. It would be a more pleasant place to bring up a family and we did intend to have children in due course. In fact, as we hadn't used contraception since getting married some five months earlier we were expecting children sooner rather than later.

'Very nice,' we said as we handed the keys back. 'We'll think about it.'

'You'd better think quick. There's only three left. They'll all be gone by the afternoon.'

The salesman showed us the remaining unsold properties on a large map.

'We'll take that one then,' I said, pointing at number 10.

'Hang on,' said the salesman, somewhat taken aback. 'Have you really considered this properly?'

'Yes,' interjected Brenda. 'We've decided to buy number 10.'

'Have you got a deposit?'

'You say you give 100% mortgages.' I pointed at a sign in the office.

'Yes, but only to people earning enough money. The house you want costs £5,900. You won't be offered a mortgage greater than two and a half times your annual salary.'

From the look on his face I could tell he didn't believe I could be earning that much. I guess that our rusting yellow Mini with the exhaust pipe held on by string and parcel tape didn't give the impression of affluence.

'Won't they take my salary into account as well?' queried Brenda.

'They'll offer double your joint salaries but that does mean that you'll have to keep on working.'

We looked at each other. Were we that transparent? A quick calculation showed that with Brenda's salary taken into account we could get the mortgage.

'Will you both be able to get to your work from here?'

Clearly this guy had been trained in the hard sell.

Within an hour of having looked at the show house we had signed all the forms and the house was ours, subject to the mortgage. It didn't all go smoothly. Initially the building society would only offer us £5,800. We nearly pulled out because of that. However, I managed to persuade them to lend the full amount and our finances were boosted by a timely win of £50 on the premium bonds.

My mother-in-law did everything she could to try to get us to reconsider. She nearly had apoplexy when we told her the price.

'Five thousand nine hundred pounds! No house can be worth that sort of money.'

If we wanted to buy a house, could we not have got something nearer to Bracknell?

That house was the first one we bought together; the first place we could really call our home. Being a brand new house we were able to put our own stamp on it, decorate it the way we wanted. We were only there five years before we upsized but in that time I repainted the outside twice. I occasionally make a detour to drive past it. The lilac tree that I saved from certain death by drastic pruning of a frost-damaged trunk is now thriving but the garden is neglected and the outside could do with a repaint. No owners will love it the way we did.

I'm Waiting, James

Julie Roberts

'Take a leap of life,' says the advertisement.

Haven't I been doing that since I was born? Six weeks early, and yellow as a lemon. My mother tells everyone she meets, especially those in a bus queue, that she had a Chinese-looking baby. That's a lie; I had blonde hair, blue eyes and I'm now six foot tall.

Being tall proved a bonus when I was queen of the high jump. I've got a dozen medals nestling in velvet somewhere in the loft.

Even my career has been a leap into the blue. I saw an ad about women in the RAF and *hey presto*, I was folding parachutes for seven years. Then a job behind a reception desk, smiling at strangers, answering millions of questions, and going home exhausted with tongue fatigue.

Finally, I found a man, and in desperation got married, got pregnant and got divorced. All in two years of unhappy hell! I'm fifty-five now and going to be a grandma in four months.

So, what's stopping me taking another leap – perhaps this time it will be my lucky day? What's the number – it's ringing. *Now stop worrying.* I realise I might be phoning some weirdo who only wants me for erotic photos. Oh dear, it's taking a long time to answer – perhaps they've got enough dollies. What a shame, I'm now in the mood for something daring.

There's another ad here: *'Lady wanted for gentleman's companion. And all expenses paid.'* If that isn't taking a leap of life, I don't know what is.

The phones ringing – it's a deep masculine voice: 'Hello, darling? Thank you for phoning. Come right round, 299, Peakeast Street. My door's on the latch.'

Bloody hell! That's an invitation any girl *should* ignore. But, as I've said, I'm no girl.

*

I'm still here. I'm sure you're relieved to know this. I'm beginning to think of you as one of my best friends. A confidante, someone I can talk to about anything. I'm in The Bell pub. I've downed two large G&Ts to boost my courage. Now I'm ready to meet Mr Mystery Man.

Peakeast Street's the posh area: big houses, long drives. Mr M's is hidden behind a high brick wall. The gate looks like Nottingham Castle's portcullis. Is he expecting a Maid Marian? I'll be a disappointment then. What a whizz sports car: sleek, black and James Bond-ish. Have I found one of Reading's multi-million-pound bankers? Great, he can pay off all my bills and set me up in a luxurious apartment. Whoopee nights, whips and chains, and a little black maid outfit wouldn't be too bad.

Sorry, am I shocking you? A middle-aged woman can't ignore the creeping years passing by.

All this excitement is giving me palpitations. Do you think it's fear or anticipation?

I'm getting the feeling you think this is a big mistake. You may be right, even the front door looks a thousand years old. And it's not 'on the latch'. So he's a lot more the cautious gent than he sounds on the phone.

OK. Here goes.

He's not worried about the neighbours. The bell's ringing

Big Ben gongs. Lordy, should I run? Don't start sniggering. I'll see this through.

It is Nottingham Castle! That's three bolts he's just pulled back. I agree with you, this is definitely one of my more extreme mistakes.

Wow! Sean Connery, eat your hat.

He's the most gorgeous hunk I've ever seen. Six foot six, wide shoulders under a *real* silk shirt and a waist I'd give my two front teeth for. I take that back, he can have the two old wisdom teeth my dentist wants to take out.

I need to take myself in hand. This has got to be the best interview of my life.

'I phoned a little while ago. You asked me to come right round.'

'Ah, yes, number 124. Come in.'

'Just a minute, I'm not auditioning for *The Prisoner* remake. You're saying there are 123 applicants before me?'

'Darling girl, you're the only one today. Fill in this form.'

Only one page on a clipboard: height, waist, leg length, *bust*? There's nothing about typing or brow soothing.

Where's he gone?

What do you think I should do? Scoot, while I can?

Na. I've taken the leap. It's too intriguing to stop now.

A green light's flashing over a door. It's opening.

'Darling, come in.' It's that voice again.

My legs are like jelly. I can hardly breathe. Will he be in a silk dressing gown, with bare legs, tanned and smooth? Smiling with kissable lips? His arms wide, waiting for me?

What fantasy world am I living in? It's only an interview.

Really, what must my new friends be thinking? I know.

I'm nothing more than a loose woman, looking for a good time. Sorry to disappoint, but when push comes to shove, I am.

Right, I'm going in.

Wow! The room's dark and candlelit, I can hear romantic Mantovani music. The bed has red satin sheets and there's a white flimsy negligee – for me? Who else? I'm the only one today.

Oh, the feel of it is wonderful. I've popped my clothes under the bed. I know. You're calling me a hussy. I'll just put that down to jealousy.

There's champagne and two glasses. Shall I pour myself a glass? Why not, get in the mood and be ready for when James comes in. Of course, this may not be his name, but Bond would expect me to be lying on the bed – dripping a few drops of bubbly between my boobs. Oh, all this surmising is heating me up. Come to me, James.

I can hear the door opening. I'll close my eyes; wait for the moment.

He's breathing heavy already.

What's he waiting for, Christmas?

'Darling, I'm coming.'

What's happened to his beautiful deep masculine tone?

'I'm waiting, James.'

'I just need to get out of my wheelchair. Brian is expecting another applicant. Will you help me out?'

*

I'm back in The Bell.

What an embarrassment. I grabbed my clothes and ran.

Can you imagine what I looked like running down the

road? I'm sure you can. Think Bridget Jones…

And to make things worse there's two young women in the ladies' cloakroom. You've heard the expression *gobsmacked*, well they were *gobdropped*. And the boxes the pubs provide are so small! But there again, they're not meant to be changing rooms.

Well, here I am, my friends, sat on a bar stool, wearing my jeans and leather jacket. I didn't bother with the bra and t-shirt. It was like a sauna in that loo.

I've got a double G&T. I'm just looking through the rest of the ads.

I know what you're thinking, but don't say a word, or I'll never speak to you again.

The Woman Who Loved The Lido
Vera Morris

'Well, Philip, will you take on the project?' Charles asked, leaning on his stick, the breeze from the Thames lifting his thinning hair, once as dark as mine.

'I can't make any promises. I'll stay in Reading for three days and give it my full attention. I can't guarantee anything more.'

The autumn sun gilded the grass of King's Meadow, where a complex was to be built. It was an important project; it would probably take four years to complete, with 1984 as the deadline. Did I want to be involved? I'd only taken it this far because of our friendship.

He smiled, looking frail. I'd known him for 30 years; he'd taken me into his firm as a newly graduated architect and our relationship matured from colleagues to friends. We stood, with a group of Reading councillors, close to a crumbling Edwardian lido. The brief was to build a hotel with sports facilities and to restore the lido to its former glory. The low, red-brick building was shabby, graffiti sprayed on its walls and scrawny buddleias cascading from the iron guttering, but I supposed to the locals it had a period charm, with its small, central tower, and two wings stretching out under a steep, tiled roof. Was it worth saving?

'I'll visit the site by myself, Charles, and let you know by the end of the week.'

He grasped my hand.

'My mother loved the lido. I'd like it to be saved.'

His mother? He'd never mentioned her before. I felt

pessimistic; the building didn't impress me, it had a melancholic and depressing atmosphere. It would be like bringing back from near death a person who had reached the end of their life. Better to pull it down and begin again.

*

I was staying with Charles at his home in Caversham, once a village on the north bank of the Thames, now a dormitory of Reading. That evening, after dinner, I decided to walk to the lido across Reading Bridge. As I approached it, the rays of the setting sun caught the red bricks, warming them to a ruby glow. Why was it important to Charles? Because of his mother? Someone told me she'd died when he was a child. I'd never asked him about her and until that afternoon I didn't realise she was still important to him.

The September evening was warm. The Thames seemed motionless. A few swans admired their images in the glassy water before gliding to their night's rest. I breathed in the languid air, feeling as though time was retreating. Even if I decided not to take on the project, a few days here, away from the pressures of London, would be welcome.

I turned the key Charles had given me in the padlock of the lido door. The entrance hall's mahogany-covered walls were bloomed by damp, and the glass in the ticket kiosk was grimy and cracked. The rectangular pool, open to the air, was far bigger than I'd expected: about 40 metres in length and 15 metres wide. The green water, which was half-way up the fractured tiled walls, was strewn with old leaves and feathers. There was a smell of rotting plants, like a cemetery urn when dead flowers are removed. Rusted cast iron columns supported the roof protecting the tiled walkway, its edges guarded by ramshackle railings. As I stepped forward, pigeons, wings clattering, rose from their roosts into the sky.

I found a chair in the kiosk and placed it at the edge of the pool. I closed my eyes, trying to envisage the future complex: how the new buildings might blend and complement the lido. I liked to absorb the atmosphere, study the terrain, immerse myself in the surroundings. This way I did my best work; the museum, the towering office block, the church, would seem, when finished, as if they'd grown organically from their surroundings.

I imagined the lido restored, full of young people enjoying themselves. I could hear the cries of the bathers as they plunged into the pool, see crystal water arcing through the air as they splashed each other, and feel the sun on my skin.

A fresh perfume replaced the smell of decay; lily of the valley.

'It used to be beautiful.'

The voice was crisp, clear and feminine.

A tall, erect woman stood next to me. She was old, but beautiful. Her oval face, with its softly-creased, pale skin, aquiline nose and large, grey eyes, was perfect. Her white hair was piled high and she wore a long, grey-silk coat, with a blue scarf round her neck.

I got up, confused, as tongue-tied as a gauche teenager. She smiled.

'I'm sorry, I didn't mean to startle you.'

'You shouldn't be in here. Health and Safety, you know.'

Why had I said that? I sounded pompous and stuffy.

She laughed, unperturbed.

'I know, but the door was open and I couldn't resist coming in.'

She looked at me questioningly.

I introduced myself: 'The site is to be redeveloped, I'm here to assess it.'

Her eyes sparkled.

'You'll bring my lido back to life?'

'It's a possibility – I was thinking it might be better to demolish it and start again… but now…'

'You can sense it, can't you? Feel the happiness, the pleasure, hear the gaiety.'

'You used to swim here?'

Her eyes widened and her hand swept the air. 'My dearest memories are here.'

Those few words startled me. Such passion.

I moved towards her, stirred by the strength of her emotions.

She backed away, eyes now full of pain.

'And the worst.'

Her hand clutched the scarf and her voice was full of fear.

I tried to speak, but couldn't.

She blinked away tears and smiled again.

'I must go. I do hope you decide to rescue my beloved lido.' She swept past me, leaving the scent of lily of the valley in her wake.

I wanted to reach out and stop her leaving. My body was frozen. Suddenly, as if a switch had been thrown, I came to life and stumbled out. In the dim light, I thought I saw her grey figure disappearing into the copse of trees that curved behind the lido. I was confused; her beauty and her contrasting moods had disturbed me.

As I walked back across the bridge, the moon's face rippled in the water of the river. I imagined her young and beautiful, in a demure bathing costume, diving into the lido pool. Who was she? Such a beautiful and distinguished woman must be known in the town.

That night I dreamt of the lido. There were smartly mortared bricks, polished mahogany and clear water lapped against gleaming tiles. From the far end of the pool a naked woman, her long hair flowing, dived into the water and swam towards me with powerful strokes. She rose, the moon's rays caressed breasts and slender arms, her perfect face radiant with love and desire. It was her. The woman who loved the lido.

I wanted to go to her but again I was frozen. A shadow passed me, stepping into the water. A naked man took her into his arms, kissed her lips and caressed her breasts. She wrapped her legs round him and they sank into the water. My heart raced and acid rose, burning my throat. She loved *him*. Him – not me.

I woke gasping for breath, the eiderdown on the floor, skin coated with sweat and my body aroused. I wanted her as I'd never wanted a woman before.

All I could think about the next day was returning to the lido that night, hoping to see her again. Not as the old woman, but the night beauty of my dream. I wanted to ask about her, to tell someone what I'd seen and felt. I thought of talking to Charles, but I was afraid he'd think I was mad. Perhaps I was.

At last night came. The town was quiet, the weather had changed, and the air was frosty; autumn had started to bite. I walked across the bridge clutching a torch. Wraiths of river mist floated over King's Meadow and there was a smell of decay. I sat on the chair, the torch beside me, waiting for her. Would she come? Would her grey eyes welcome me?

The moon's reflection crept over the black water and a chill ate into me. I looked at my wristwatch. Ten past one. She wasn't coming. I got up, stiff with cold. Something moved in the pool. My chest tightened. Below the surface a shape darker than the water floated towards me. I switched on the torch. There was a black froth on the surface of the pool. Slowly the shape took human form. Triumph filled my head – she was coming to me! Breathless and impatient I bent over the pool, shining the beam onto the rising figure.

There was a rush of water and a scum of bursting bubbles released a fetid smell. The form rising from the water was a man. His dead eyes stared at me. A gash in his throat – like a pair of furled lips, spouted black blood. He waded towards me, water pouring from his body. He reached out a bloated hand, its rotted skin hanging like apple peelings.

I couldn't breathe. I couldn't move. He came closer. The stink of death overpowered me. His slimy hand touched my cheek. My legs buckled under me and I collapsed into his outstretched arms.

I came to shivering with cold and fear. I cowered into a ball like a frightened child. Where was he? I scrambled up, my heart pounding against my ribs. The torch was glowing where it had fallen. I picked it up and flashed the beam round the pool. The man had gone and the moon with him. The water of the pool was still, the evil stench replaced by a trace of her perfume. Had she saved me? Who was the dead man? He was not her lover. He was taller and stronger than the man she'd held in her arms. Who were these people? Was I ill? Had I a fever? Was I mad?

*

The next morning, I summoned up my courage. 'Charles, have you a photograph of your mother?' I asked.

He moved to a bureau, and took out a silver-framed photograph from a drawer. He handed it to me.

'It's the only one I have of her. My father destroyed all the others.'

My hand trembled as I took it from him. It was her. Young again, beautiful, bewitching, with hair piled high, smiling at me.

'She was very beautiful. Can I ask what happened to her? Did she die when you were young?' He didn't reply and I sat down. Breathing was difficult.

He sat down opposite me, his spaniel eyes full of tears.

'No. I don't know what happened to her. She ran away… with a man, when I was ten.'

He looked embarrassed.

'That's why my father burnt all her possessions. I hid the photograph. I couldn't believe she'd leave me. She loved me so much and she knew I adored her. I think of her every day.'

A man? The lover in the pool?

'What was her name?'

'Charlotte.'

He bit his top lip, as though trying to keep control of his emotions.

'Your father? When did he die?'

'Two years after she left.' He hung his head. 'He committed suicide. In the lido. He cut his throat.'

I closed my eyes and shuddered. So that's who the man was. The rotted corpse who'd tried to take me with him. I felt sick to think she'd been married to him. I hoped she and her lover had found happiness. I wouldn't let her husband win. Charlotte's wish would come true. We sat in silence.

'Why did you want to see her photograph, Philip?'

'I just wanted to see the woman who loved the lido. I'm accepting the project, Charles.'

During building excavations, the skeletons of a woman and a man were discovered in a grave near the trees behind the lido. An inscribed wedding ring proved the woman to be Charles' mother. The man was unknown. She was reburied in the nearby graveyard of St Peter's Church. Seven months later the grave was opened again and Charles was reunited with his mother.

Charles left me all he possessed and I made his house my home. As I sit at his desk, Charlotte smiles at me from the silver frame. Can you love a woman you have never met? Never touched? Never kissed? Each night I fall asleep hoping to dream of her again, but she never comes.

IN THE TOWN

In This Town

Claire Dyer

there's a waterfall of cloud
and I'm sixteen, kissing a boy
who'll leave on a train heading west.

I'm working in this town,
buying typewriter ribbon
in Broad Street, its

Etch A Sketch of shopfronts,
its skyline's mismatch
of ages. In this town

swans' necks snow-curve
as they cruise
the gunmetal river,

windows blaze brickwork
and tall chimneys back at us.
In this town are buskers

and a buffet of languages.
Someone's planted flowers
in hanging baskets.

I am waiting for my children
to be born in this town.
I remember them as commas in my belly.

They visit occasionally
from distant places, bringing
new people in the car with them.

In this town what changes
casts long shadows. We say
the word home to one another here.

After John Piper's tapestry 'Reading Townscape' which is currently held in Reading Museum.

Number 21 To Nowhere
Andy Bennett

Matt looked out of the side windows and watched the bus pull away from the station and head off on its journey to Lower Earley. There was a weekend's worth of things in a backpack beside him on the front seat.

'Oi, mate,' came a gruff voice from somewhere, 'give an old guy a hand up these stairs.'

Matt turned to see a scruffy old man with scruffy grey hair dragging himself up to the top deck. He looked very unsteady and was bouncing between banisters as the bus moved.

'You going to help me or what?' said the man, still struggling and panting.

Matt was a bit surprised the old man hadn't stayed downstairs as he wasn't looking so capable of the climb, but stood up to help. The man was also dragging a large suitcase, which added extra thoughts about why downstairs wasn't a better choice.

'Where do you want to sit?' Matt said to the man now ahead of him.

He was panting himself due to the incredible weight of the luggage.

'I think I'll sit up here in the front. I likes being able to look out.'

Matt dragged the dead weight of suitcase the few feet to the chair.

'Thanks for that, mate. I feels so much lighter not having to carry that around with me.'

Matt really wasn't surprised, it was unbelievably heavy and he was pleased to put it down.

'No trouble, sir.' Matt replied.

'Sir. Now that is gallant of you, not like them toe-rag students you get, don't even stand up to give an old guy a seat… Although I suppose you is a student… but may be not such a toe-rag, eh?'

'No, I guess not.'

Matt sat down and looked out of the window at the shops as the bus headed through town.

'Well, thanks anyway, you is a gent to an old man. I would lay my hat down… if I had one.'

He nodded and turned to look out of the window.

Matt looked at the road ahead, and then rubbed his right shoulder as it hurt quite a lot from moving the suitcase. *Oh well*, he thought, figuring at least he'd helped someone.

The bus continued and Matt's mind began to drift into his own thoughts.

'How long you lived in Reading?' came the gruff voice into his right ear. He turned to see the man staring at him.

'About two years,' Matt answered.

'Two years? Me, I've been here 72 years, man and boy. Born here, grew up here, worked here, all me life. Now, I could tell you a thing or two about Reading, seen a few things me. Things that would make your toes curl.'

Matt still really didn't know what to say. 'Good,' he replied.

'Good indeed.'

The man paused.

'The first thing I could tell you is this.'

He paused again and then waggled his finger randomly in the direction of a building on London Street.

'Do you even know why Reading is indeed called Reading?'

'No,' Matt said, a little reluctant to be talked at for his whole journey.

'What are they teaching in that university if you don't know that? Well, let me tell you,' he leant a little closer.

An unholy odour wafted from the man's mouth as he did so, which made Matt recoil.

'As not many people know, some 250 years ago Reading was just a small village. It wasn't even called Reading, some just thought it was nothing more than a bridge over the Thames, but it had a name, somewhat due to its relative stature in the area, of Lesser Bracknell.

'As you also may not know, with your fancy phones and internet, people made bread outside of factories back then. They needed actual flour, made from actual wheat, made into bread by actual bakers. There was a lot of all that round here. They were all bakers there.'

He pointed at a small row of shops on Christchurch Road.

'So, to celebrate this, the Lesser Bracknell council held a festival. The Great Breading Festival of 1786.

'It was an amazing event, held right there,' the man pointed randomly at the university site, 'in Whiteknights. Bakers travelled from all around. Bringing their finest. All forms of bread were represented: white, brown, crusty, soft, sliced, non-sliced – everything. It was all there.

'Everyone who went said it was magnificent, and that the

world had surely never seen so much bread in one place at the same time. And that probably that much bread would never been seen again.

'The council of Lesser Bracknell wanted to celebrate this success, and at that very meeting they decided to change the town's name. No longer would they be just a river crossing. Now they would be remembered as the breading capital of the world.

'They thought hard and long, and then finally, like geniuses, they had the new name – they would call it Breading. But that sounded a bit rubbish so they shortened it. So, there it stuck, from that day forth: Reading – as a reminder of past greatness.

'So, that is how the name came about. And don't you forget it. Anyway, this is my stop.' He pressed the button to stop the bus. 'Help me off, would you?'

Matt did as he asked, trying to use the other arm for the suitcase this time.

'Thanks, mate,' he said, 'you is a true gent. Don't forget the legacy, it is my gift to you.'

The man stepped off the bus. Matt watched him cross the road, struggling with the massive suitcase, and then sit down at the bus stop on the opposite side of the road next to a woman. He saw the man turn, waggle his finger in the woman's direction and then start talking.

Matt smiled and watched the scene, as the man headed into the distance behind the bus.

In Ancient Days

Charles Whittaker

In ancient days when Reading Abbey
Was less barren, derelict and shabby,
Pilgrims came to get pardons
In Forbury Gardens
And paid tithes, 'til the monks became flabby.

Gorbachev Invades
Susi Dillon

'What in God's name is going on?' I asked my husband.

We were standing on the pavement outside the Broad Street Mall in the late spring of 1990 and the noise was deafening. The high-pitched noise was everywhere, in Laura Ashley, in Sweeny Todd's where we bought our pasties, the fish shop in Smelly Alley, the camera shop and now all around us on the street.

The noise set my teeth on edge, like fingernails sweeping down a blackboard.

'Maybe it's a civil defence thing,' said Peter, scrunching up his eyes at the sun shining for once on a Saturday.

'Maybe Helmut Khol has found some more V2 rockets,' I offered.

'That's not funny,' Peter looked at his watch. 'This has been going on for over an hour now.'

'Well, where's the police then? Nobody seems worried,' I said.

The flow of shoppers parted around us as if we were the Israelites crossing the Red Sea. Several threw us strange looks but moved on without saying anything.

'The Russians, I bet the Russians have decided to invade, the buggers,' Peter said.

'Really? Why would they attack Reading?' I rolled my eyes.

'Maybe this is just the start of wearing us down.' Peter grabbed my arm.

'You can't be serious,' I protested.

'Well, something's definitely going on. Come on, let's get a coffee.'

He led the way through the Mall and upstairs to the small café we usually frequented.

A young girl was idling behind the counter. Her jaws worked furiously at an enormous wad of bubble gum, her tongue deftly flipping it from side to side in her glistening red mouth.

Peter waved to get her attention.

'Do you by any chance know what that noise is?' he asked.

Thick glasses perched on the end of her pudgy nose and a sprinkling of freshly squeezed pimples stood out like the Mountains of the Moon on her red cheeks.

'Beats me,' she shouted back.

'It's doing my head in.' Peter rubbed his temples.

'Can we have a couple of coffees?' I said.

'Yeah,' she chomped down hard on her gum and dribbled some tepid coffee from a pot brewing on a hotplate behind her into two mugs.

'That'll be two pounds fifty,' she said.

Peter handed her the money while I grabbed a couple of packets of sugar.

'I don't understand why the police aren't doing something,' I said.

The girl's eyes flickered back and forth between us. 'Don't think the police can help you.'

'What would you suggest then?' asked Peter.

'Dunno, doctor maybe?' she said in all seriousness.

'I'm getting a migraine,' Peter said and took our coffees

to the nearest table.

'We first heard it when we were leaving the multi-storey car park,' I said by way of explanation.

*

A group of boys clustered about the entrance to the coffee shop and the girl was quickly losing what little interest she'd had in our predicament. She blew a large pink bubble and sucked it back into her mouth where it burst with a snap.

'I only just noticed the noise but it was feckin' loud,' she said.

Simpering, she moved off to give the boys a better view of her breasts and left me feeling like an idiot.

I sat down next to Peter. I viciously ripped the tops off the two little sugar packets and dumped one into my coffee.

'I couldn't get anything useful from her.' I said and handed him one of the packets. 'Silly cow hasn't a clue.'

Peter stared at the smear of cold coffee remaining at the bottom of his cup.

'She's just as bad as that guy in the camera shop. He looked at me as if I'd lost my mind.'

'Well, you shouldn't have called him a prat when he laughed at you.'

I stirred my coffee vigorously and took a sip. It was disgusting.

Peter shrugged. 'He was lucky I didn't call him something else. Are we finished here?'

I had hoped to spend an hour on my own checking out the new summer clothes in Heelas while Peter scoured the books in Blackwell's, but he looked quite green now from the deafening screech.

'It'll keep until next weekend.' I patted his hand. 'Let's go home.'

'Thank Christ,' he muttered.

We abandoned the café and took the lift up to the top floor car park.

'It's as loud in the lift as it was on the pavement!' yelled Peter. 'How the hell can that be? What are they up to these bloody Russians?'

'Once we're in the car it's bound to be better.' I said and scrambled out of the lift.

It was no better in the car.

Peter jammed the gear stick into first.

'As soon as we're out of Reading it should stop,' he shouted as we sped away.

We flew out of the multi-storey, whizzed past the old bus terminal, hit the bend at Cemetery Junction on two wheels and headed up the A329.

The horrible noise was all around us.

My patience finally snapped.

'Can't you do something?' This was the line I always fell back on in times of mega-stress.

'Well, what do you expect me to do?' Peter fired back, gripping the steering wheel so hard his knuckles turned white. 'Downing Street must know by now,' he said. 'Russian tanks are probably all over London and will be grinding their way into Berkshire any minute! Bloody Gorbachev!'

'It's not the Russians!' I said. 'We'd have heard something on the BBC.' I cranked up the radio to the sound of Kylie moaning about tears on her pillow. 'Check the boot because I'm at the end of my tether with this noise!' I shrieked.

Peter glared at me. 'Oh, for Christ's sake I'll pull over and have a look if it will make you happy.'

I couldn't believe we were having a fight about a noise. 'Don't shout at me!'

'I'm not shouting at you.' Peter banged the steering wheel with a fist. 'This bloody country is going to the dogs. Where's the police, the army, the air force when we're being invaded? I bet they're all in the pub having a good time. I wish I was in the pub having a good time!'

'That's your answer to everything, isn't it? Go to the pub!' I yelled.

'Well, what's wrong with that?'

'I suppose it means you're not having a good time with me!' I finally burst into tears.

'I didn't say that!' Peter shouted.

'Oh, it doesn't matter. Just shut up and do as I ask, will you?'

I wiped away my tears only to discover my expensive waterproof mascara was now all over my cheeks.

Peter wrenched the steering wheel to the left and jammed on the brakes. Small stones pinged off the bottom of the car as we jerked to a stop.

'Okay, okay! I'll check the bloody boot!'

He got out and slammed the door.

The noise was gone.

Peter opened the boot, closed it with a thump and climbed back into the car.

The noise was back.

'There's nothing in the boot,' he shouted.

'It's you!' I cried.

'What?'

I pointed my finger at him. 'It's you making that noise! It stopped when you got out.'

'It can't be me, I haven't got anything...'

He sat with his mouth hanging open, a funny look on his face. He fumbled underneath his jacket and pulled a small black box out of his inside pocket. A red light on its top was blinking manically. Peter pressed a little switch on the side and the light blinked twice and the screaming stopped.

We sat in blessed silence for a minute or two.

'When did you get a pager?' I asked quietly.

He cleared his throat and gave me a sickly grin:

'The office gave... this is a new procedure... must have malfunctioned. I forgot I was carrying it, sweetheart.'

'You forgot,' I whispered.

'Who would have thought such a little box could make so much noise?' He gave a strangled laugh and his face flushed bright red. He shoved the offending pager back into his pocket, well out of sight.

'Do you realise half of Reading thinks we're mad?' I fumbled for a pack of tissues in my handbag and rubbed at the streaks on my face, trying to stifle a laugh. 'A Russian invasion of Reading indeed!'

'It's not beyond the realm of possibilities you know.' Peter adjusted the rear-view mirror even though it didn't need adjusting.

'No tanks on the M4 then?' I asked.

'Nope, not today.' He flipped the indicator on, gunned the engine and pulled out into the traffic heading for Wokingham and Bracknell.

'But could I make a wee suggestion, just a small change to our routine?' He asked tentatively.

'And what would that wee suggestion be?' I knew what was coming but I wanted to hear him say the words.

'Perhaps we could forgo shopping in Reading next weekend?' Peter gave me a brilliant smile.

'Good idea, and perhaps the weekend after as well, sweetheart,' I replied.

The Nerks

John Froy

In the Easter holidays of 1960, me and Paul hitch-hiked
down to Reading. Some cousin of his had a pub there, Betty
Robbins and her husband Mike. We didn't bring our birds;
there was no room for them, apparently. We just set off
hitching one fine day. The weather was balmy, barmy, but we
weren't getting any lifts, so Paul hid our gear, two guitars and
the Elpico amp, behind a bush. He was the bright one, Paul,
I failed all my O-levels. Then the lifts started. They were
short rides then, not like the heyday of hitching in the 70s,
more a leftover from the war and conscription when the
armed forces hitched everywhere. There was a lot of goodwill
to help people standing by the road, and we got there in the
end.

The Fox and Hounds, we found, was over the river in the
village of Caversham. And we were sharing a single bed – no
wonder there wasn't room for Dot and Cynthia. Our
landlord came in to wish us good night! But we were working
in a pub, serving drinks behind the bar, and having a few
ourselves. Paul was only seventeen at the time. This age thing
kept cropping up with us, especially when we got to
Hamburg – Paul was in trouble for some prank and it
became a real problem; George was actually thrown out of
the country when they found out he was playing at the Star
Club underage. We kept quiet about Paul's tender years,
didn't want any trouble when the coppers looked in at
closing time. *He was just seventeen, you know what I mean.*

So what did we do in Reading? I hardly recall. Suppose I

could get out of the clouds and ask Paul, but I'm not sure where he is at present. He's as famous as ever, superstar going incognito etcetera – as I would be if I ever came down to earth. I'm John, by the way. I guess we just worked behind the bar, lunchtimes, evenings. We went into town one day, walked over the bridge over the dirty Thames… I remember now, we were in a coffee bar in Broad Street with these girls we met, talking about Eddie's crash. I mean it had just happened. Eddie Cochran had died! Crashed into a lamppost in Chippenham. They were driving back from Bristol on the A4, his girlfriend and Gene Vincent in the car packed with their gear, and he was killed. They would've come right through Reading.

Then we went into some municipal gardens with this enormous black iron lion in the middle from the Afghan wars. We were by the prison, man, Reading Gaol, where they incarcerated Oscar Wilde for being gay – queer, bent, we said then – and had him picking oakum – whatever that is – for a year. They wore the poor guy down, broke him, killed him. We saw his gravestone in Paris later on, an amazing thing by Epstein, that's right, another Epstein, Jacob not Brian, covered with all these red lipstick kisses on the pale stone. It blew my mind. You'd want to be remembered like that, like you'd made a difference somehow.

So we worked for a week, wore our socks off behind the bar. We asked Mike if we could play, and he said we could, on the last night. We called ourselves The Nerk Twins for the evening. In Berks. OK, it's not The Silver Beetles, or Beetals, or even the Beatles – that was just around the corner, in August to be precise, when we were being booked for

Hamburg. Jesus, we arrived there in the red-light at dusk, a young group hardly formed, and we played all night in the clubs for three months, that's what made us into a band, you know.

Anyway, we did these posters for the show and put them on the lampposts:

THE NERK TWINS APPEARING TONIGHT BY HER MAJESTY'S SPECIAL APPOINTMENT. FOX & HOUNDS, GOSBROOK ROAD. 8PM. SHARP. They had some of my drawings on them, but none have survived.

We were opening with *Be-Bop-A-Lula*, but Mike said it wouldn't work in the pub. Start with the instrumental *The World is Waiting For The Sunrise*, he said, *then* do your Gene Vincent. He knew about showbiz, he'd been an entertainments' manager at Butlin's, so we did that. Paul played the melody, I played rhythm, and Mike said it was perfect. Paul was really impressed by this fella, he influenced his music through the years.

Of course we did *Summertime Blues* as our tribute to Eddie Cochran as well. We sat on barstools in the tap room and played to twenty people, and it was really great, man. It worked, you know. Mike asked us to do Sunday lunchtime as well, then we had to leave straightaway, hitching back to Liverpool because Paul had school on Monday. I didn't go into the art college much then.

John Lennon and Paul McCartney did hitch down from Liverpool to the Fox and Hounds, Caversham, in the spring of 1960. They performed as the Nerk Twins on 23rd April. It is believed to have been the only time the two of them played together in public. Look out for those lost posters in your attic, folks, they might be worth a bit now.

Full Throttle

Rob Wickings

'… And with less than a minute to go there's still no sign of Barry Steele! What on earth is going on with the Reading Rockets? The last race of the night, at the moment when they could take the league title and their star rider is nowhere to be seen!

'No… No, wait, here he is! I don't know if there was a problem with his bike but here he comes, folks! The question now is, what state of mind is 'Steel Bar' Barry Steele in, with everything to play for and the future of his team poised on what he does over the next 90 seconds?!'

I hate that announcer. He makes such a bloody drama out of everything. I know that's his job, but it's bloody distracting. It's not like I don't have enough on my plate as it is.

The bike's heavy and feels sluggish. That'll change once I crank the motor. 30 seconds from now. Then the old instincts will kick in. Then it's me and the track and nothing else matters.

Who am I kidding? This time, *everything* matters.

'15 seconds to go, and Steele takes his place at the line! The race is on, folks. But what must be going through the mind of Rockets' manager Roy Breaker? What just happened in the team compound?'

I know exactly what's going through Roy's head right now. We are two of the five people that know what just went down at the back of the garage. I can see Roy now, at the compound line, face pale as milk. Behind him, almost in the shadows, are the other three. Gary Priest, loan shark, gangster, villain with a capital 'V' and his sidekick and muscle, the man who only answers to the name Spike.

Between them, arms caught in Spike's bone-grinding grip, the one person who shouldn't be here. The one piece of leverage Gary Priest knows he has on me.

Dammit, Ma, I told you not to open the door to strangers.

Time slows in those last few seconds before the wire goes up. You find you have time to settle, to check out that first bend, to find your line, to scope the riders to either side. Your senses sharpen, everything jumps into focus. The tingles start in your fingers and toes. There's a sharp taste on the tip of your tongue. You're more alive in those seconds than at any other time.

So you spot things that you might otherwise miss. Like the grin that Sammy King throws at me as I glance to my left. The lead for the Slough Stormers, our bitterest rivals. His smile tells me everything in a flash. He's in on this. He knows.

Five seconds. My hand drops to the starter switch and twists. My bike sputters, then roars. She's alive under me in a moment, urgent, ready. Sammy does the same. The grin hardens, turns animal. We both have scores to settle, and he thinks this race is the moment he wipes the board clean.

I turn away, meaning to check my line, but there's one face I'm drawn back to. Ma, gritting her teeth against the pain as Spike wrings her forearm like a dishcloth. If I could, I'd jump off the bike right now and go for him. But by the time I got across the track, he'd have snapped her neck. I take a second, just to look at her, to drink her in.

And she looks at me, with those bright blue eyes, and she shakes her head. A tiny bit, but she knows me, and she knows I'll spot it. The message is clear.

Don't. You. Dare.

The klaxon blares and the wire rattles up. I let the clutch go, and the bike leaps away. The most important race of my life is on.

'It's easy,' the Priest said, five minutes and a lifetime ago. 'All it takes is one mistake. One little fumble on a corner. Skid out a bit when you shouldn't. You're the best speedway rider I know. You can make it look real. But you don't get to win this one, Steel Bar. Not with the folding I have on Slough to take the title.'

I jump at that, even with Ma in Spike's grip, even with the revolver hanging in the Priest's hand. One of my hands is a fist, the other a claw. It's only Roy, with his ex-rider reflexes, that catches me in time and hauls me back.

'*No,* Barry.'

I've never seen him like this. Roy Breaker, Rock of the Rockets. The man who brought us to the brink of our greatest victory. I hope you never hear your hero sound like that. So scared.

'Listen to your boss, Bar.'

The Priest doesn't jeer or sneer. He's not like the thugs you see in Valiant or Lion. He doesn't need to put on a front. He knows he's already won.

'This goes one way. You can't just be disqualified. You have to lose. You can make it as close as you like. To be honest, I'd prefer it. It needs to look good. Not forced, you know? But Sammy King takes the trophy tonight. Sorry, but you were just too good not to bet against.'

Roy has a hard time holding onto me after that. But God bless him, he does. And he sends me onto the track, even though losing now will break his heart.

So somehow, in the next minute, I need to figure out a way to make all this horror come right.

First corner. I dig in, slew round and cut inside Sammy, blocking his line. He's a good rider, but predictable. He hasn't changed his starting strategy since the first time we raced. We hit the straight, and I put the hammer down. Five seconds to the next turn. Thinking time.

I have to lose, or my ma gets broken to bits. I can't lose. All the fans, my team mates, everyone has put their heart and soul into this moment, this race. If I let this one go, our best chance in a generation for the team to be something special vanishes like diesel smoke in a hard wind.

But who would blame me, really? It's obvious that the pressure is on. The contest is so close at this point. Like the Priest said, one little fumble. One mistimed corner. Just enough to let Sammy King through. No one would know.

Except me, and Roy, and Ma. And that's what it boils down to. None of us could come back from a moment where I gave in. I don't think I could get back on a bike again, knowing that I gave Gary Priest his payday. That I handed the trophy to Sammy King.

That they broke the Steel Bar.

No. That's not happening. Not today.

I jink right round the second corner, and let my back wheel slide six inches wide. It fishtails. I can feel the power in the back wheel die, emptying into a sideways slide. Sammy sees the gap and takes his chance. He roars past and grabs the lead.

Just like I want him too.

I have a plan. It's a spare, desperate thing. Barely more than an idea. It depends on so much happening at once. On the people I love reading my body language, knowing what I'd do.

It probably won't work. But it's all I've got. And for now, it depends on Sammy King being the rider I know so well.

I stick to his back wheel through the next two laps, dodging left and right. Making it look like I'm trying to find a space. Ignoring the huge gaps he leaves on every corner. The crowds will be screaming at me now. Willing me to shunt him aside. I can't hear them over the roar of the bike, but I know what they're saying. If I was on the other side of the barrier I'd be doing it myself.

Last lap. I drop back a little. Just enough to let Sammy think he's free and clear. He wants this to look good, though. As if he's won it honestly. He takes a nice tight line into the first and second corners. It's the best I've seen him ride all season. Almost graceful.

The last straight. The long one. I see his shoulders drop a fraction. In his head, he's won this. Any second now...

There. He can't help it. He needs to gloat. So he glances back. And in that half-second, when his eyes are off the corner, I smoke him.

Sorry, Sammy. I've been holding out on you. I pour on the power, that little fraction I've been holding back for this moment, and barge right up to him. His attention should be on the hard left turn a second in front of him. But it's all on me. He doesn't even see the corner until his front wheel bites the cinders.

He loses control, the bike bucking under him like an angry girlfriend. Dirt sprays up and his handlebars twist out of his grip. He pancakes, hard, the bike bouncing away from him. He rolls to a halt, eating grit, one arm twisted underneath him in an ugly double knot.

He's behind me now, forgotten. I have another job, and I hope to God this works.

I win the race without even thinking about it, screaming past the tape at full throttle. The crowd goes crazy. This should be the greatest moment of my life. I can't even think about it, because the next ten seconds will change everything. There will be no victory lap. I'll never lift the League trophy.

But I will find peace, even if it's in a jail cell.

I keep the throttle open and blast towards the compound. The thing about speedway bikes? No brakes. If you lose control, your best option is to fall off and pull the spark plug out of the engine once it's slid to a halt. I kink and swerve a little, just to make it look like the steering's locked.

At nearly forty miles an hour I roar through the safety tape and into the team compound. Gary Priest is dead ahead, his face twisting in rage, barking an order at Spike. But his henchman can see what he can't. Spike is already getting out of the way. He drops Ma's arm, just like I knew he would.

Ma, she sees it. She knows what I'm doing, and her role. It's a simple part to play, and she times it dead on.

Just as Gary Priest realises, the rage dissolving to a skull-grin of realisation, Ma shoves him with all her strength right into my path. Speedway bikes aren't heavy, but I'm going at race speed when I hit him. My tyres are viciously treaded and that hard spinning rubber finally finishes the job I've been wanting to do since I first laid eyes on his ugly mug. It takes the smile right off his face.

Then I do lose control, as the back wheel skids on something belly-soft and slick with gore. With less than a second before I hit the back wall, I fling myself sideways, off the bike. It runs into the brick and bounces. The drive chain snaps and sprays hot metal. One burning fragment cracks the back of Spike's head, and he drops in his tracks. The engine screams, then coughs and dies.

It's quiet for a while. I might have gone deaf. I think I've broken my left leg. It shouldn't bend like that at the knee. I'm covered in track-dirt, and I stink of oil and blood. A shadow falls across my face. I look up and see Ma holding her arm. Bruises dapple the flesh of her bicep, and I suddenly want to throw myself at Spike. Then I try to get up and my leg reminds me what's happened and the pain is a lightning strike that knocks me on my back.

Ma is at my side. She unbuckles my helmet and winces at the state of me. Then she smiles, and I know that it's going to be alright.

'You silly bugger,' she says, and lays a cool palm on my brow.

Somewhere behind me, the crowd noise is building, and there's the whoop of a siren. Later, I'll have to face the music. For now it's me and her, and I won the race and I'm the champion.

And that's the only thing that matters.

Many Happy Returns

Hannah Piekarz

Three o'clock, he'd said. And where was he? The Boar's Head probably.

James shifted his position and rubbed the mud-red brick dust from his hands. He leant back again and scanned the passing traffic for a white Escort hatchback. He was hoping for two flashes of inspiration. One, reassurance that Simon, his snapper, wasn't enjoying a pint of Best while he loitered in the vicinity of Jackson's Corner, and two, that he could find his story. Sure, the new library opening wasn't going to make the front pages of the *Evening Post*. Not unless Princess Di showed up. But this old Duke guy? Who'd heard of him? Wouldn't even make the community pages without a picture. Where was Simon?

James discarded the stub of his cigarette into the gutter with a well-aimed flick. Stashing his ten Benson carton, he felt inside the inner pocket of his shiny grey suit for his Dictaphone. He could record the atmosphere. Take vox pops from the crowd waiting for the Duke to arrive. As he approached the gathering on the corner, he could hear what sounded like an excited party. It was, in fact, little more than a high spirited bus queue full of football fans. Festooned in the scarves and hats of the Royals, the seven o'clock kick off was the closest this bunch would get to royalty today. Via the number 17 to Elm Park.

Moving on to the library, he peered through the smoked glass doors which remained shut tight. Screened off, nobody came out to greet him. This was becoming a non-story. He sat on the brick wall, regretting not being a court reporter on days like these.

'What's the scoop?' Simon slapped him on the back, snapping him out of his reverie.

'You git. Leaving me here, missing all the action. Duke's been and gone, library's closed. Where were you?'

'The IDR's murder. Seems everyone's going into town this afternoon. Taken me 20 minutes from Tessa Road. Seriously, have I missed it?'

'You've missed nothing. I was thinking about shooting off. There's no human interest in this piece.'

'You'll find one. Do you want to head up and get a bite to eat?'

'You've been watching too much Cagney and Lacey – that's a great idea. I'll just nip over the road to get some money.'

They entered the banking hall of the Abbey National intent on serious business. They silently surveyed the queue that snaked up and down behind the red velvet rope. With a nod of the head, James indicated the plan and they hopped on through to the room at the side.

The only sound was the buzz of the fans from the automatic machines that were the size of tumble driers. The room was empty of people, too, just like the launderette.

'See, you just sail through and don't even need a passbook.'

James pressed his bank card into the slot and withdrew his hand like a nervous postman. The machine spat back a beige tenner, which James swiftly pocketed.

'Enough for a wild week. So where are you taking me?'

'I thought we could try McDonalds.'

'Why not?'

The marble chess-board floor of the restaurant marked out their next battle, which line to join. This was a welcome delay, though; it gave them time to ponder their meal choice as they read the boards. It all sounded exotic to James.

'So much better than the Wimpy Bar, don't you think?' Simon lowered his voice.

James wasn't listening; he had his ear tuned in to the conversation going on between the mother and daughter ahead of him in the queue.

'Can I have cake, Mummy?'

'No, I think you need to hold a birthday party here for that.'

'But it is my birthday. Will you ask them, Mummy?'

'I don't think so...'

'Well then, can I have cake at the library?'

'Umm...there might be, we'll have to see.'

'And will the Duke give me a card?'

The mother sighed, and James strained to hear more. 'We've already been through this. He'll give you your very own library card, not a birthday card. Because you're 12 now. And then you give him the flowers as a thank you.'

'Seems like an unfair deal to me.' The girl kicked her feet.

'Excuse me,' said James. 'I'm terribly sorry, but I couldn't help overhearing – you're going to be at the library opening later, yes?

'Um, yes?'

'James Chandler, *Evening Post*. We'll be covering the story.'

He fumbled to find his press card, without success, and instead held out his hand to the mother. She shook it with the lightest of touches.

'Sue Flood. And this is Lizzy.' There was a pause as Lizzy stared up at him, almost blushing.

'And this is Simon, who'll be taking pictures of the birthday girl later.'

Simon nodded.

'Oh, dear. We've been trying to explain the celebration isn't for Lizzy's birthday, it just happens to coincide with the library opening. We were getting the message across.'

'As long as I can have a card, some cake and a gift from the Duke, I'll be happy.'

Mum looked awkward. '…I think.'

James smiled. 'When you have your own library card, you can choose a gift every time you visit.'

'Can I help you?' the girl in the maroon cap behind the counter slurred through her braces.

Sue waved her hand to pause the conversation and order food. With the meal delivered and a hungry child to feed, they were soon lost in a helter-skelter course of brown trays, paper straws and the rush to bagsie a spare table.

James and Simon ordered, and not wanting to incur the eat-in charge, left with a brown paper bag apiece. They crossed the road, and James felt as if he was in New York City. This was cool.

They walked along Market Place, pausing at the pet shop to watch the rabbits in the window. As they walked away, the noise of chirruping canaries followed them along the pavement.

'Feels like a wasted morning. An unrecognisable Duke, a spoilt child. This big new building with little more than a load of shelves in it. What's the point?' He felt like a rebel, still slurping his Pepsi as he walked.

'Umm. You've got to see the bigger picture.' Simon unwrapped the transparent paper of his Filet-O-Fish. They reached a bench and sat down to eat.

'Mmm?'

'Inside every book there's a story.'

James cast him a look to see where he was reading this lolly-stick wisdom from. 'You what?'

'Your story's got to be about all of the stories inside the library.'

Simon painted the picture with his hands.

'Through this building, we've got access to the whole world. Tales from the past, the future...'

James chewed on his plastic straw and worried about the effect that the E numbers were having on his friend.

'Right. I do see your point. Yeah... but can my story have lots of great pictures too? Are you coming?'

Reading Reflections

Charles Whittaker

I

Hanging on the abbey stone,
bejewelled spiders' webs
shimmer in morning light,
flutter as if to draw their victims in –
just as St. James the Greater's hand
stretched out to passing pilgrims
in need of comfort and forgiveness
from the first martyr of Our Lord.

II

A net of tracks and tarmac streets
now spreads out from the town
drawing residents and visitors alike
to tree-lined avenues of shops
and into tracery patterned domes
of air-conditioned halls.

They come, a multicoloured throng
that chatters and laughs its way,
down Broad Street into the waiting jaws
of John Lewis, Debenhams
and the Oracle shopping centre,
watched by old unshaven men,
cold-bummed amid discarded fags
on concrete council seats.

The river passes tall offices of glass,
where faces sip at paper coffee cups
peering at computer screens,
sifting your claim, and maybe mine
for that incident last week
where Oxford Road meets Zinzan Street.

Beneath the trees in Forbury Gardens
and watched by a giant metal lion,
couples spread out on patchy grass,
munching soggy sandwiches
they brought from home
in silver foil and plastic bags,
blind it seems to Henry's abbey, Pugin's church
and Scott's red prison walls beyond.

Down the road, beside the still canal,
they once sent Chocolate Olivers
by Appointment to The Queen
out to a long gone empire.
Now it's superstores of sofas,
DIY and toys, all made in far-off lands.

III

This was the earth besieged by Essex
in April sixteen forty-three,
to take the garrison of King Charles,
and where again, in eighty-eight,
Dutch William marched his troops
from Caversham, down Broad Street,
to crush James the Second's Irish
and set democracy in stone.

After Dark

Gareth Cahill

'So, where we meeting? I should be getting into Reading in about two hours,' Sam asked over the phone.

'Wild Lime on Friar Street isn't too bad,' I replied, checking my watch.

Sam would be getting into town just before seven and he'd want something to help line his stomach. 'Food is pretty decent there, too.'

'Sounds good, Matt, but where is that?'

His signal was beginning to cut out, so it was not the best time to try and explain where Wild Lime was.

'Erm, I'll text you. See you at seven.'

It had been 15 years since Sam was last in Reading. While Wild Lime was a common name around Reading now, and a popular venue, it had been Cape when Sam was last here. Or was it Varsity or Barracuda? Luckily I had a couple of hours to remember what Sam and I had known it as, otherwise I'd have to give him directions from the 'new' Reading station. That would be another change Sam would not like and I'd rather deal with that over a beer or five.

It's not change itself that Sam doesn't like; he's lived in more different places, and countries, than anyone else I know. Sam doesn't like the idea of *Reading* changing. I quizzed him on this once, about 10 years ago, and all he said was that seeing the changes would tarnish his memories. By his tone I could tell it was a delicate subject, so I never brought it up again.

*

'Newt and Cucumber!' I exclaim from the back of the number 14 bus taking me into town.

A few people look round at me. Another couple glance out of the corner of their eyes at me and snicker at the strange man at the back of the bus shouting out random combinations of amphibians and vegetables. I'm half tempted to shout out 'Frog and potato!' as I text Sam Wild Lime's old name, but decide against it. They probably wouldn't get it.

I don't know why I even decided to sit at the back of the bus upstairs. Most of the time I can't be bothered with the queuing along the aisle waiting to get off at the end, but that's during rush hour. Now it's a bit quieter I guess I'm reliving my youth, although the bus then was the 65 and it took a shorter route around Woodley rather than every twist and turn the 14 takes now.

*

It's amazing what changes around you, what you don't notice, or simply forget about. Other times you take the memories and move on, accepting it. Although when you see your home town for the first time in a long while, you see every change.

*

'Dude,' Sam said, hand outstretched ready to meet mine before it became a back-slapping hug. 'What the hell happened? I came out of the station and everything is gone. Everything!'

I smile and pass him a beer and gesture towards a table. I had warned him that things would be different last time we met for a quick drink in London a year or so back, but seeing is believing. I see it most days and am still in awe of how different it all looks.

'I know mate,' I said. 'That's a whole chunk of our history gone.'

'Yeah. Most days working at the bingo hall. Then most nights down in Bar Oz.'

'I think my liver is thankful that's all flattened and way back in our past now. It'll be good to see it all finished though, eventually.'

'I bet, I bet,' Sam said, wiping his mouth on the back of his hand. 'But where's our teenage years gone?'

He had a point. A very good point. Our formative years were disappearing in apartment blocks and shopping centres. Where once we used Friars Walk as a cut-through to the back of the bingo hall or were dragged into C&A by our parents, everything had changed. Give it ten more years and most people would be reminiscing about the time they went on the "Zombie Run" through the disused shopping centre before the station redevelopment finally claimed it. All we have are memories of releasing stink bombs from Fun 'n' Frolics in the lifts of the car park that is now, probably, Debenhams in the Oracle.

'Ahh, what did we ever do before the Oracle?' Sam asked.

'I think we generally just met up at, and hung around in the old Virgin Megastore in the Butts,' I replied, racking my brain for memories of misspent Saturday afternoons walking around town not doing very much. 'It's a bank now.'

'What! A bank?' Sam cried, the beer loosening his vocal cords.

But his yell simply joined the night-time buzz of voices, music, laughter and singing that made up a typical Friar Street bar.

'Where do kids meet up when they get off the bus now?'

'Not a clue! The Woodley buses don't even go to the Butts now. They're allowed to the station and that's it.'

I knew that would almost send him over the edge; more of our childhood history gone, more changes to the town we call home.

'You should come home more often, Sam. It's good to catch up like this, rather than over a fleeting pint at Paddington between our trains. Or better yet, you could move back? It's been 16 years since the accident.'

The accident. The one topic we had both avoided as best we could for as long as possible, and I was taking a chance bringing it up now. Me, Sam and his girlfriend Kate, had been walking back from a friend's house, after watching England beat Germany 1-0 in Euro 2000 when a drunk driver had mounted the kerb and ploughed into us. Sam and I escaped with a few broken bones but Kate wasn't as lucky. She died at the scene.

Kate was effectively the sister I never had. Our parents had been close friends for longer than either of us could remember. We met Sam at secondary school and the two of them hit it off straight away. They were a classic example of childhood sweethearts. Her death hit Sam hard; everywhere around him reminded him of her. I guess he moved away to avoid the constant reminder of what they had shared, I never dug any deeper when he replied, 'Because I have to' when I asked him why he was going. He probably hasn't been back until now so that he could hold on to those memories as tightly as possible. Was his being here now a sign he was ready to move forward? I had to risk it.

'Kate wouldn't want you to live in the dark like this, mate. Your family's still here, as well as a lot of our friends.'

Sam looked at me directly, eye to eye. I couldn't read him. He was either going to storm out of here and disappear for good, or punch me and then go. Despite the noise of the pub, the silence stretched out between us, drowning out anything else, until he sighed and looked away.

'I know mate, I know. It's time for me to live again. But work is backed up and I was lucky to get this time away. Besides, where would I live?'

'Don't think that would be too tricky, there's flats and apartments going up everywhere! RG1's...'

'Wasn't that the club where you could be found most Fridays? Just down from the bingo hall,' Sam said, wagging a finger as he took a swig from his beer. 'Ah-ha! No, it was the one that used to be the bingo hall before it moved to the Top Rank Suite!'

'That's the one. That's been flats for years. Almost all of the old clubs are gone. Level One is now several apartment blocks and everyone's old favourite, Utopia, is becoming an Ikea!'

'Well, I guess you need one locally. We had some nights in there. Do you remember the foam party where Jimmy decided he'd dive across the dance floor?'

'Oh God, yeah! When we left A&E after the sun had

come up 'cos the idiot got his hand sliced open.'

'Yeah,' Sam laughed. 'That's the one. When all he said afterwards was "and that's the reason why they don't allow glass on the dance floor"! You ever see him, or any of the others?'

'Rarely, well, apart from Smithy. He might join us later, depending on what time he finishes.'

With the advent of Facebook and Twitter it's so much easier to keep up to date with the people you knew once upon a time. Sometimes in more detail than you actually care for.

Some people you hear nothing from until their name appears in the paper, or someone shares a link about them, for one reason or another. Some representing club or country in the sport they've loved since before they met you. Others, sadly, have the length of their sentence written next to a very unflattering photo. Thankfully these are few and far between; you just skim read for what they have done, coupled with a shaking of the head and a sigh.

*

'So,' Sam started. 'We having another in here, or are we moving on to another old haunt that now has a stupid new name?'

'Let's grab another in here,' I replied. 'It's your round anyway.'

Sam chuckled as he made his way through the typical Saturday night throng of people. I reckoned it gave me a couple of minutes' breathing room to work out our next steps for the night. Truth be told, I've not been a town centre "night owl" for some time, with the odd exception of one too many after work, the obligatory wetting of babies' heads or watching a sporting event.

It's not just Reading that has changed, I have too. Normally, I'm much happier just heading to a local pub of a weekend. An easy walk home, kebab van on the way and much less of a hangover the next day. But this isn't a normal weekend. Sam's back for the night so we are making the most of it before our bodies take more time to recover from a hangover than from minor surgery. Time to relive our youth, as best we can, as if nothing's changed.

Another 'one' in Wild Lime turned into two or three more as Sam and I reminisced and reminded each other of our most embarrassing moments throughout school. Sam was never able to live down the fact he was found sleepwalking on a Sixth Form trip. Naked. Sam also reeled off several of my misdemeanours that I had forgotten about. The alcohol loosened my lips and made me regale Sam with yet more embarrassing stories of more recent years. Should I ever get married, Sam probably has far too much on me for him not to be my best man.

We set the world to rights, as only half drunk people in bars can do. Most of this focused on Reading – what we'd change, what we'd change back from how it is now, and what should never be changed at all. John Lewis would have its name changed back to Heelas. HMV would reopen on Friar Street. The Allied Arms would never be allowed to shut down.

'You know there used to be a pub under the Broad Street Mall?' I asked.

'The where now?' Sam replied. The issue of the naming

of that shopping centre had already been picked apart by the two of us.

'You're right. I guess it was called The Butts Centre when this place was open.'

'Was there? Whereabouts?'

'On the side where the market usually is. I never really noticed it before, but there's grating on the ground and if you look closely enough, you can see that there's steps down and actual space there. I think that was where the main entrance was.'

'That would have been awesome. How'd you find out about this?'

'It was on *GetReading*, what used to be the *Evening Post* before they decided to go completely digital.'

'Ahh, that would make sense,' Sam said. 'I always thought that it was just ventilation or something to do with the tunnels under the town that run from The Sun to the Abbey.'

'Urban myth, mate,' I was sorry to say. 'That would be awesome, to have real beer run tunnels under the town, but too many people have come out against the possibility of them actually existing.'

'Damn. Anyway, what was this place under the Butts? What happened to it?'

'From what I know, it was called The Target. I think it was the victim of health and safety. Not enough exits, or too many fire risks so something like that. Great live music venue apparently.'

'Guess we're not the first generation to see major changes then, especially in the night life.'

'That's for sure. Probably not the last, either,' I said,

finishing my drink. 'Right. C'mon, drink up. Time for us to make a move.'

'Great, where we off to next?'

'Probably the only place that's not changed in Reading for a generation at least, and probably won't change for several more.'

Sam gave me a bemused look as he put his jacket on, arm swinging slightly wide, almost hitting another person carrying a round of drinks. No damage done, and more impressively, no drink spilt. Sam issued quick apologies and turned back to me.

'Well?'

'The After Dark Club, Sam. The After Dark.'

The Biting Hunt
C.J. Smith

There were no other seats left, so Vanessa sat next to Adam. She'd never spoken to him, but she'd heard him say he liked Lord of the Rings. When there was a lull in the meeting chatter, Vanessa nudged Adam gently.

'So, who do you think was the better ring bearer: Frodo or Gollum?'

He swivelled his head and peered at her. 'Most people start with "hello".'

'I'm not most people,' Vanessa said, though she wasn't sure that was true.

Adam smirked. 'Is this your first year at Reading?'

Vanessa snorted. 'First year out of the nursery, the way some of these professors make me feel.'

'I know what you mean.' Adam regarded her as if she were an important document. Something to take time over, to absorb. 'I'm Adam.'

'I know.' They shook hands, and Vanessa felt a tingle travel up her spine. She liked Reading better already.

*

'I can't see!' Vanessa laughed as Adam pulled the Panama hat down further over her eyes.

'You don't need to see anything. Just experience the wind blowing gently through your hair.' He ran his fingers through her chestnut strands. 'Lovely hair it is, as well.'

'You are so silly, but thank you.' She felt something plop onto the hat and yelped. 'What was that?'

'That, my dear, was a conker. Just as well I protected you

with my hat.'

She smiled. 'My prince.'

'Yes, well, it does get tiresome amongst you commoners. I almost didn't come to Reading, you know.' Adam pulled the hat up and peered into her eyes. 'I could have gone to Oxford.'

Vanessa had applied there, but had been rejected. 'I'm glad you're here with me,' she said.

'Are you sure?' he teased, taking the hat back and twirling it on his finger.

'Yeah.' Vanessa traced his strong, sure jaw, and bit back a groan. He was more myth than man to her. 'Every time I see you, I feel like a kid on Christmas morning.'

His eyes widened. 'Oh, Van.' They kissed, and settled into each other's embrace.

Vanessa gazed at the Forbury Lion in the distance as Adam's stubble grazed her face. Her hunt was over now.

*

'I didn't enjoy myself at our dinner,' Adam said, eyeing her as they settled on the bench by the River Thames.

Vanessa sighed, and watched as some canoes went by. 'And I suppose that's my fault?'

'Well, it's not your triumph, my dear.'

Vanessa pinched the bridge of her nose. 'Right. Okay. Tell me how I'm supposed to make this better then, Adam.'

'You could start by being a little more considerate of me, darling.' Adam glared at her.

Vanessa slid away from him on the bench and let the tears slip down her cheeks. She was grateful her eyes were covered by the large black sunglasses she'd taken to wearing in case Adam got in his lecturing mood.

At last he sighed, and pulled her into his arms. 'I'm sorry I get like this sometimes. I love you, Vanessa.'

She leaned into his hug, but felt the cold wind off the water embrace her more tightly.

*

They did a macabre dance amongst the stuffed animals; taxidermy, not Build-a-Bear, each avoiding the other, with glass, fur and teeth as the barriers between them. Tired of the dance, Vanessa stalked him like a predator while Adam pretended she wasn't there.

By the Bayeux Tapestry Vanessa ventured, 'This is lovely.'

Adam grunted. She inched closer to him, and rubbed his upper back. Instead of the purr she longed for, he hissed.

'I'm trying to look at the tapestry, Vanessa. Do you mind?'

She examined her hand, for she felt sure he must have bitten her, but it was only pale and trembling. She held it as if it were her own child. 'Why do you hate me?' she whispered.

Adam didn't answer.

*

'I simply cannot endure this anymore, Vanessa. You bitch, and you whine. You're manipulative. You're paranoid,' Adam said, glaring at her as if she'd killed his pet.

Vanessa could say and do nothing but stare in numb silence as he circled her atop the hill like a shark. But no. A shark couldn't survive outside the water. He must stop soon.

She turned with him as he continued to circle her, feeling

like a little plastic ballerina in a music box, but this music was not sweet and light, but a thundering funeral dirge, and his bitter jabs as he listed her every fault made her dizzy with agony.

'Adam,' she whispered. 'Please stop.'

'No,' he snapped. 'You've talked so fucking much. You have reached the end of my patience, Vanessa.' He clenched his fists, and she sucked in a breath.

Adam grabbed her upper arms and pulled her to him. She wrinkled her nose at his sour breath.

'I hate you! Get out of my life!' he yelled, digging his fingers into her flesh.

Shark bites, she thought, and cried out.

Adam shoved her back in disgust and marched down the hill. Gawkers snickered at Vanessa. No one came to her aid.

Bit of Sunday entertainment for them, I suppose.

Vanessa stepped delicately down the stone stairs, though tears blinded her, and glanced blearily at the Forbury Lion, then at the rapidly forming red welts on her arms. She was the hunted. And yet she must endure. But how?

Beating The Reaper
Bob Billing

The only certainties in life are death and taxes. The government want taxes every year but most of us don't survive our first encounter with the Grim Reaper.

Except that the score is now one-nil to me.

I'm an old, tubby chap with most of the usual complaints such as diabetes, high blood pressure and eyes that need pretty strong spectacles. I'd been trying to lose weight and was suffering erratic drops in blood pressure. I'd even made an appointment to have my GP investigate.

Then everything fell apart at once. I'd gone to bed early, I woke up at about 2am, went to the loo and couldn't get back to bed. In fact I couldn't even stand up.

My wife lifted me, breakdown truck fashion, and I staggered into the bedroom then collapsed in a heap on the mattress. At this point a little red light came on in my mind. *Uncle Bob, we have a problem.*

This has just gone from the annoying side of getting old to something serious and is heading rapidly for life-threatening. It's ambulance time.

Those guys are good. My wife had hardly put the phone down when there were blue lights outside and a chap in green overalls inside sticking wires on me.

Something was deeply wrong internally. It was time for a trip to the Royal Berks in Reading. The only problem was the first twenty yards. I couldn't stand up long enough to walk, the passage was too narrow and had too many right-angle bends to get me in the wheelchair.

Time for me to make a quick engineering decision. I had my wife put a dining chair in the passage. I sat on it, breathed a lot of oxygen, and let the drip work. Then I stood up, got about three paces and let someone shove the chair under me again. All I had to do was repeat until I was outside.

Then I was on the trolley, being loaded into the ambulance, or at least one of them. The performance so far had run the first one out of drips and oxygen, so the second one has come as a sort of in-flight refuelling tanker.

I decided that I must keep awake, must be able to answer questions. There was no fear, just a hard, cold determination to beat this, to keep my body functioning as long as I could so that the doctors had time to do something.

We rolled to a stop, for a moment there was cold, blue morning sky, then I was on a table in crash and people were working on me.

Blood group? I'm B, rhesus positive. I know, I was a donor for years.

That was the problem. There was blood where there shouldn't be any, and a shortage where there should be lots. They sent for 'two units cross-matched' ready to start topping me up.

What's wrong was quickly obvious, or to be accurate bleeding obvious. Somewhere down in the depths there was a hole in my guts and I was bleeding to death internally. My haemoglobin count had set a new record low, and my skin had gone the colour of old piano keys.

I was beginning to drift away, climbing a long flight of steps, and at the top there was a light. I saw a door, and beyond it I heard music. On the other side of the door there was a party going on. People were eating and drinking, playing music and making beautiful things. The door was opening for me, someone was asking me to come inside, join the festivities that had been going on from creation and will go on forever. All I had to do was step through that door...

I turned back, slowly descended the steps, and picked up my body again.

It's only much later that I realised that I'd had a near-death experience, stood on the threshold of the next world and returned to the lands of the living.

I'd faced the Grim Reaper and defeated him, a bent scythe and fragments of a shattered hourglass on the floor were all that was left of his presence.

I'd made it. Now it was time for the doctors to fix me up.

Step one was to transfuse a lot of blood, enough to keep me going until step two.

Step two was called endoscopy. They slid a fibre optic probe down my gut and tried to see what was wrong then fixed it. Think of it as a hybrid of drain rodding for people and the Battle of Britain.

They gave me some dope, so I wasn't quite awake, but I wasn't really asleep either. Then they went in. The gist of the conversation between the surgical team was something like this.

'Right, we're going in!'

'Roger, Skipper!'

'Duodenal ulcer at ten o'clock! Ready to inject.'

'Right ho, Skipper. Oh, wizard shot sir, you've got the blighter!'

'Ready to cauterise? Firing now!'

'Bang on, Skip!'

'That's it chaps, return to base.'

It wasn't quite like that, but I was sedated which may have confused matters.

They put me back to bed with a big sign saying 'Nil By Mouth'. That wouldn't have been too bad, but following the dogfight in my bowels earlier every burp came up flavoured with smoke. The glass of water they finally gave me hours later tasted better than the finest Chablis.

Slowly a sense of euphoria crept over me. I was alive. I'd faced death and defeated him. I'd walked to the gates of heaven and turned back. I slept fitfully, tangled in monitor leads.

Nothing would ever be the same again. As dawn broke two geese flew over the hospital, honking to each other. Their sound was the song of life, life which I had found again, life to be savoured in all its myriad details.

The God Of All Things

Juliet England

By the time I turn the corner into little slip road where the pharmacy is, I'm already worried. It looks dark and shut up.

I scurry along, cursing my lack of organisation. The snow which has swathed Berkshire today must have caused it to close early.

When I get there, I'm confused. The place clearly *is* shut, yet the regular pharmacist, a man I've long admired for his calm, respectful nature in the face of dozens of pensioners, all wanting their piles cream at the same time, is inside. He is in a blue anorak and jeans, talking to a young couple. I knock on the door and pull a pleading face while mouthing 'Let me in?', and he opens it. Inside, it's gloomy, in stark contrast with the daytime's harsh strip lighting, giving me a vague sensation of intruding, of being a burglar.

'Am I too late?' I ask, still on the step.

'What do you need?'

'Just my gluten free bread.'

He jerks his head towards the shadowy interior and I step inside. He walks back behind his counter. On it is a small plastic beaker of yellow, sticky-looking liquid. The pharmacist (Asian, middle aged, neatly trimmed hair not allowed a centimetre past his collar, half-moon glasses, smiley) pushes it towards the girl (pale, long dark hair) who downs it in a single swig, as though drinking for a bet at a bar, before replacing the little empty transparent cup on the counter. It feels as though it should be refilled at once, like a shot glass.

The pharmacist walks round from his side of the desk to

let the girl and her companion out and she hugs him briefly before slipping out into the freezing night with her male friend.

I have been waiting in the shadows, watching silently by a shelf of discounted mouthwash and verruca cream.

'Methadone?' I ask.

He just smiles weakly and tilts his head slightly to one side. What did I expect? For him to whip out the girl's medical records?

He says something that I don't catch. So I explain that I can't hear, adding that although I have prepared as though for a polar expedition I have forgotten my hearing aids, before demanding he finds a pen and paper to write down what he is trying to tell me.

I grab it and start scribbling – before realising that he's not the one that needs anything writing down.

'Oh, of course, *you* can hear,' I smile, and we both laugh.

Biro flying across the page, the pharmacist writes that he has driven back from his home in Harrow to give the girl her prescription, having closed at lunchtime because of the snow.

I stand there gaping.

'*You drove from Harrow*? To come back and open up again so she got her prescription – why?'

My eyes have attuned to the half-light, and it is easier to lip-read now.

He is too polite to say 'Well, duh', instead the words hung unspoken in the air. But he's clearly loosened up a little on the old patient confidentiality front, in his exasperation.

'Well, you know, injecting. It's dangerous, yeah? Dangerous. It's Friday night. If she doesn't have the medicine she must wait till Monday. I didn't want her injecting. All morning I was calling her, to tell her to come early. That we were shutting for the snow. Ten times, no reply.'

And there is the merest hint of exasperation in his voice, enough to show that, after all, this man may be a hero, but, the Lord be thanked, he isn't a saint. He is human.

When I ask (quite shamelessly) if there's any chance of picking up a prescription for myself while I'm there, he says 'no, I'm not doing that for you now. Take your gluten free loaves, bugger off and come back on Monday'. He's too polite to say it in those terms. But he does shoot a 'Don't push your luck, mate, enough good deeds for one day,' look.

I leave him to drive all those snowy, dark miles back to Harrow. I don't hug him, but I pump his hand, holding on to it a nanosecond longer than strictly necessary.

And I feel so cheered that, in a world of horrors - of Jim Davidson live in Aldershot, of First Great Western into Paddington and of Katie Hopkins being paid to hate people fleeing war who perish on the high seas, someone is prepared to drive all that way – and back again – *just to give me something to write about.*

I am practically dancing back towards the bright lights of Church Street, snow crunching like hard caramel under my boots, swinging the plastic bags with the bread in.

I am skipping over the ice, making up ridiculous songs as I go.

Oh, I've never been kissed
By a pharmacist
But I could have kissed (never been kissed)
That pharmacist.

I'm going to go for an unplanned cup of tea now, I decide. And, the hell with it, a chocolate brownie while I'm about it.

When I next go back to the chemist's after the weekend, the pharmacist's grin has the strength of a lighthouse beam. I've written up the incident as a letter for the *Evening Post*, and it made star letter. (Local papers, eh, desperate places. I should know. I used to work on one.) Has he seen it?

'Krishna will sort out your prescription,' says the woman behind the counter, nodding towards him.

'Krishna – isn't that a Hindu god?' I ask, thrilled to learn his name. 'Who is he the god of?'

She moves her head in his direction again.

'All things,' she says, grinning. 'He is the god of all things.'

Painting With Fire
Bob Billing

The stage lights are low, the lava flow in the middle of the set glows a malignant red, the band plays urgent, throbbing music.

Dick Whittington is clear of the lava, Alderman Fitzwarren is clear, Whittington gives me a hand signal to say King Rat is safe, the rest of the cast are moving downstage.

Key in, selector on.

Everyone is at least four feet away from the pyro devices.

Turn key, green light on.

Finger on the big, red button, the weight of responsibility like an iron crown.

FIRE!

I hear a muted pop from the scenery, the stage begins filling up with thick smoke.

Count... nine... ten. Next selector. Fire!

I see every face in the audience, wide-eyed in the sudden orange glare.

Next, two selectors. Count two, three, four. Fire!

There is a stinging concussion and the whole backdrop vanishes in a sheet of white flame.

Key out, selectors off.

Listen as the audience's shocked silence explodes into wild applause.

It was my first show, and it had gone perfectly.

*

We had chosen an unusually startling ending to the pantomime, *Dick Whittington*. Instead of killing King Rat, we had decided to blow her (we were staging a lady rat) to bits spectacularly in an underground volcano. This meant firing six pyro devices in quick succession on the surface of a fake wood and canvas lava flow, which was glowing red thanks to a couple of simmering tungsten lamps down in the depths. And that in turn had meant my retraining as a stage pyrotechnician.

*

One grey morning a few months before the show, I headed for the Backstage Centre, a complex of workshops and performance spaces at Purfleet, just off the river crossing from Dartford. I rolled up with a dozen or so other hopefuls, and we were ushered into a huge theatre space, empty except for a couple of rows of chairs. There we were introduced to Lincoln Parkhouse, our instructor, a friendly, genial character with an impressive history of providing spectacular effects for stage, screen and live performance. He introduced us to the various types of flashes, bangs, smokes and things that make amazing noises when burning, then turned to safety.

This was a very important part of the course, in fact the main reason for holding it at all. Stage pyro effects are devices that can burn hot and fast, and do it right next to both cast and scenery, so the risk of setting fire to the theatre or putting the star in an ambulance is very real.

To prove that even major broadcasters can get it wrong, and as an object lesson in what not to do, Lincoln showed us a video clip of an effect that went badly adrift on air, injuring the presenter who was sitting only inches from a device that was fired by mistake.

The moral of the story is very simple. Firstly make sure

that everyone on stage knows where they have to be and what they are doing. Secondly whoever is firing should not press the Big Red Button unless they can see the device that they intend to fire.

A quick lunch and then it was time for all of us to get into groups and do some rigging, each group putting together a small display, while being quizzed on the devices we were using and how we were setting them up.

Most of the effects that we used were ready-made devices that only needed the firing cables plugged in, or for some of the more exciting ones the connections were made using a crimp tool designed for telephone installers.

We were also given a smoke pellet, some gun cotton and an igniter, and told to make something to light the pellet. The igniter is a tiny blob, about the size of a match head, that explodes to order when you push the button. The trouble is that it is tiny, too small to fire the pellet, and so you need something else that will burn hot and get the pellet going.

It wasn't me that did it. Honest. It was definitely someone else who put the pellet on top of a pile of gun cotton, pushed in the igniter and fired the lot. The gun cotton exploded and launched the pellet, without igniting it, into a graceful parabola that ended in the middle of the next team's setup. That is how we learned about the danger of tamping explosions. If anything gets in the way of an explosion, that thing is going to move, even if you don't mean it to.

Finally, we all got together to set up the big show. This was both to give us experience of working as a larger team, and to let us handle some top-end equipment, the sort of thing used for spectacular, professional displays.

The result was amazing. Flashes and bangs of all colours filled the room, line rockets whizzed overhead on wires, and long, rippling sequences of sparks fell from high in the rigging.

*

Back in Reading, it was time to plan the pantomime. The easy part was the front of stage sparkles for the first musical number and two flashes which were to go off when King Rat did a magical spell.

It was the volcano that loomed larger in my mind. I wanted to give the director a sequence of firings that would paint the idea of a volcano erupting explosively. Hours of poring over device data sheets and a long phone call to JustFX later, I had a plan of sorts.

The idea was to fire two smoke cartridges to form a thick cloud, then let two flame pots flare up to light the cloud from inside, and as they burned out fire two EFS cartridges to create the final explosion. This would give a slow build up to an eye-popping finale.

The EFS (also known as the Robotic) is a wonderful thing. The initials stand for Electrical Fault Simulator. They are normally used to generate the shower of sparks that happens when someone shoots at a robot on screen, or the TARDIS misfires, but in our case they would create the effect of the volcano exploding. The problem was that the roof of the theatre at Shinfield is rather low, and the lighting rig is only about nine feet above the stage. A lot of calculation later, I knew how to place the devices.

So far so good. The next problem was that the volcano

had to be moved on stage during a very short blackout. That meant connecting four separate firing circuits, two wires each, in a couple of seconds and in total darkness, which in turn meant handling an eight-pin plug without breaking it.

Then it was down to the detailed design work, and briefing the cast. The volcano was in fact built around a slide. King Rat went in head first, slid down a ramp out of sight of the audience and landed on a mattress where two stage hands grabbed her and pulled her clear of the volcano. Meanwhile, Dick Whittington, standing on the volcano, would see her get clear and do a little victory wave, which was my sign that she was safe. The whole cast would then set off downstage, and when everyone was four feet from the devices, I would put the key in and fire.

All I had to do was connect up, and that meant some very carefully synchronised action. Standing backstage as the show got close to the volcano scene, I pulled the safety caps off the cartridges, and held them up to show the stage manager and his assistant that the volcano was ready to go, and that they could begin to move it. Lighting blacked out, the band played creepy music and the children dressed as rats scurried around in the darkness. I sprinted round the backstage space until I was behind a join in the backcloth, pulled open a little trapdoor in the stage and ran out the cables. Seconds later, the volcano arrived in front of me, but on the audience side of the backcloth, and the pins on its bottom surface dropped into holes in the stage, locking it in place. Working by the light of a dim head torch, I reached through a gap in the fabric and plugged in both the firing cable and the power to the lights.

Then it was an even quicker sprint back to the firing panel to do a rapid circuit test, check all the lights were green, and then wait for the moment when King Rat went head first down the slide.

Look for Whittington's signal, key in... And the rest is history.

The final reward was one word in the NODA review. They said, 'Pyrotechnics: brilliant!'

Cold Harvest

Richard Chalmers

The ion suspender above Adria sparked in the misty dark as it lowered her towards the ground. It kept a constant tingling pressure on her shoulders and the back of her neck.

Adria surveyed the terrain as she went, her visor display updating with each metre of her descent. Air content: 12% oxygen. Ambient temperature: -47°C. Nothing could survive down here. That was why she wore the suit. Power was holding steady at 84%. It was old kit and the aging batteries never held more charge than that. Their ship, the *Kerberos*, would keep her topped up via the tether.

The comm-unit in her ear fizzed and a steady male voice asked, 'Adey, how're you doing?'

'Fine, Captain. Almost down. Something wrong?'

Fzz. 'Don't think so, but watch out for glacials.'

Adria braced herself as her feet disappeared into the ash and snow. It went up to her knees before her studded boots scraped the ground.

She looked around. It was like the gardens were inside an unshaken snowglobe, a thick haze defining its limits.

'Adey?' her captain fizzed in her ear.

'I'm down. Keep an eye on the sensors for me and I'll watch for snowmen down here.'

Fzz. 'Roger.'

The line closed with a click. Moments later, the ion suspender vanished.

Adria reached behind her back and felt around the tether with her clumsy gloves. It was still secure. She could begin.

Adria's team had located a graviton source here, in a town called Reading, one among the thousands of glaciated ruins on Earth. For once the *Kerberos* had run well all the way here, and no one had pursued them. Nothing was going to stop her bringing that source home.

Adria watched her knees shunt snow out of the way as she walked – lumbered, really – through Reading's Forbury Gardens, where no one had trod for decades. She was leaving a trail that was impossible to miss, the weight of the tether making her movements even less graceful.

Thankfully the snowmen – the glacials – were blind. They could only hunt by sensing heat in their surroundings and would latch onto anything that felt warmer than the environment. Literally *latch*. They weren't malicious, but they were mindless and strong. They just embraced their victims until they froze to death.

The haze was starting to grow thicker as Adria's movement lifted ash back into the air. If the snowmen somehow felt her through her suit, she might not see them coming until it was too late.

Adria was looking for the lion. That was the feature closest to her arranged drop point. Once there she could head directly east towards the graviton source. Her suit's sensors weren't sensitive enough to detect its signal until she was almost on top of it, so she was relying on what she'd memorised from the *Kerberos'* scans. What her suit *would* do for her once she found a point of reference was overlay a map in her visor, as even digital compasses had been useless since the pole shift. Once she had that she could go the rest of the way blind if she had to. The lion had better be…

Adria's boot cracked against a rock and she tumbled. She went straight forward and felt her helmet bounce off something in front of her. She spun and tumbled into a heap in the snow.

'Son of a…!'

Fzz. 'Adey, are you all right?' The Captain's voice was ringing in her ears. Her helmet was padded but she'd gone into that thing hard, and now her brain was rattling about inside her skull.

'I'm fine,' Adria snarled. 'It's getting hard to see down here, but I think I found the lion. Or its plinth.'

She felt around for grip under the piled snow and pushed herself up against the side.

The Captain breathed a sigh of relief.

'Good. How has it held up?'

Adria pressed her hand against the statue and leant outwards. She looked up, but all she could see was a mist of ash and snow.

'I can't even see the lion.'

Fzz. 'That's a shame. I was hoping for some pictures,' the Captain quipped.

'Come down and join me,' Adria suggested. 'You can stand on my shoulders.'

The Captain's fizzled laugh filled her helmet. 'Next time, Adey. Update your display and keep…'

Fzzzzz.

Adria paused. 'Captain? You there?'

Her display suddenly came to life. She had a path laid out before her eyes in ethereal orange.

Fᵤᵤᵤ '…tether. I'm trying to reset it. Copy?' *Fᵤᵤᵤ*.

'Captain, I can barely hear you. If you're reading me, I'm proceeding to the graviton source.'

'Adey? I can hear you. I think we're back. Don't proceed. We'll abort and retry. I've had to reset the tether. Something's wrong with the power transfer. Your battery isn't receiving charge.'

Adria shook her head before remembering that he couldn't see her.

'If we wait, one of the merc groups will just swoop in and take this from us.'

Mercenaries were the bane of their existence. No one else was sanctioned to be in the area, but sanctions didn't stop everyone. Sometimes mercs would shadow them all the way to their targets and then take the prize right out from under their noses.

There was silence on the other end of the line, and not because it had gone dead again. The Captain knew she was right.

Fᵤᵤᵤ. 'Okay, but only because we might not make it back to Azure City without it. How long does your suit have left without recharge?'

Adria peered up to check her display. '12 minutes.' This was going to be tight.

'I want you back in 10.'

'Then I'll need to disconnect the tether. It's just dead weight now.'

Adria reached behind her and started to fumble with the cables. After a click and a hiss the tether dropped lifelessly into the snow. She was as free as she was going to be in this suit. She set off at a march.

'Captain, I'm moving again. Retract the tether.'

Silence. He was considering again. 'Alright. Just let me know if you want me to come out with the spare.' *Fzzzzz.*

Adria began moving as fast as she could. The Captain wasn't kidding about not making it back to Azure City. Without enough gravitons the *Kerberos* would fall out of the sky. Gravitons were vital for keeping the fleets, and the cities they called home, aloft. They'd only need a fragment of this one to refuel the ship, and the rest would go to the city.

As Adria went around the edge of the lion she heard the tether retract. It clanked and groaned as it sank into the snow and dragged along the ground. Watching it vanish into the ashen mist left a lump in her throat. She swallowed and kept going.

Adria's display showed her exactly where to expect the bandstand. She skirted around it, running her gauntleted hand across its bars. More icicles dangled from trees either side of her, which loomed out of the airborne ash like frozen goblins.

It was beautiful and eerie in equal measure. There were speakers inside her helmet that delivered sounds from external microphones, yet these were perfectly silent, except for the crunching of her footsteps. No wind, no sound, no life. Earth would never lose its splendour, even in death.

The ground rose into a shallow hill on her left, but the elevation of her target remained constant at her level. She veered right.

Adria checked her power again, self-conscious now that it was finite. The battery was draining steadily. Her suit was too heavy to carry with just her own strength so most of the power it afforded was spent just on helping Adria lift it.

But she couldn't slow down. She was getting closer. The visor display was coalescing as she approached the source. Ten metres, eight. There was another feature ahead of her on the display.

Adria stopped beside a low wall that surrounded what appeared to be a fountain. Through her visor all she could see was a cone of snow that had gathered around it over the years, but the fountain was clearly superimposed on her orange visor display. She kicked aside enough snow to see the wall itself. The fountain must have been ancient. It seemed to be made of assorted uneven stones, like a geological collage.

Her display finally showed signs of gravitons, so now came the hard part. The scavenger crews had never found a piece bigger than six inches across and the graviton field they emitted could easily be several metres wide. This was a problem. If the source was buried in snow, the eight minutes remaining on her display might not be enough to find it.

Adria did a lap of the fountain, which was about five metres in diameter. The source was definitely here, and close to where she'd first approached the fountain. She knelt down on the side of the wall and plunged her hand under the snow. Her fist punched solid ice and she rolled her eyes. What had she expected? Water, at -40°C? Six minutes left. Okay. She pushed both hands into the snow and shoved a huge swathe aside.

There it was. The graviton source was staring right up at her from below the ice. Metal blacker than obsidian, blacker than coal.

She drew back her fist again and punched the ice with the full strength of the suit.

She flinched as tiny shards exploded against her visor.

Her comm unit fizzed in her ear again. 'Adey...' *Fzzzz* '...and six minutes left,' the Captain pressed. 'How are...?' *Fzzzz*

She punched the ice again.

'A little snag. The source is embedded in the fountain, which is frozen solid.'

She straightened up. The ice was too dense. She was chipping away at it, but she'd never make it through in time.

'Captain, I'm going to have to cut it out with a pistol.'

Fzzz '...tive. Did you say th...?' *Fzzz* 'Abort. We'll...'

This time the comm unit didn't fizz. It was just dead.

Adria watched helplessly as her display dimmed and then went out completely. That wasn't just the battery; it had still been forty percent full. It must have been damage from the fall against the lion.

'Shit.'

Adria wasn't going home empty-handed. She could use her thermite pistol, but that could attract glacials from hundreds of metres away. Although, if there were any nearby, surely they'd have responded to something by now? Just by running through the snow she was generating heat.

She could risk it. They needed this source.

She unclipped the holster, flipped out the pistol and set it to its lowest setting.

'Here goes nothing.'

Adria aimed and pulled the trigger. A white light flew out

of it, striking the ice like a bayonet of lightning. Adria looked around nervously as the ice began to melt. Nothing, no movement. She held her finger on the trigger.

The ice was sinking in on itself as it contracted, releasing steam. Soon enough the source floated to the surface. Adria let go of the trigger and reached in with her free hand.

She loved just looking at the sources. The way they reflected light was so beautiful, so unearthly.

Adria stood up and pocketed the source. As she turned away she reset her weapon and secured it on her hip. At a guess, she had three minutes left to retrace her steps through the snow. She was going to make it.

There was movement in the fountain.

Adria froze.

Her side was still facing the fountain, but if she ran now, she could make it. She could go, right now, and she'd be okay.

Something was filling the silence: a shallow, clacking wheeze.

Adria tilted her head ever so slightly, just enough to see...

A glacial was rising out of the snow. It was the size of a man, but made of living ice and crystalline sinew and bone. Frozen ash slipped from its jutting shoulders. The noise it made sounded almost like breathing, except snowmen didn't breath, as far as Adria knew. They only hungered. How long had this one laid here, starving, buried, before she used the thermite pistol?

Adria bolted.

Snow exploded behind her as the glacial landed. It had

jumped clean over the fountain and missed her by inches. She'd never have moved fast enough with the tether still attached. Adria looked down and immediately saw the path she'd made through the snow. She ran, the suit moving as fast as she could force it, groaning horribly in protest.

Over the suit all she could hear was her own panicked breathing and thumping heart. Where was the glacial? Right behind her? They could laugh at them, call them snowmen, when they were on the surface ten miles below, but when they were breathing down your neck...

Adria couldn't even see the bandstand yet and already she was getting tired. The suit was getting heavier. How low was the battery? With the display dead she had no idea. If it ran out of juice she was done for.

There! The bandstand! But, oh God, the suit was slowing. She wasn't going to make it.

Adria unstrapped her pistol, spun, and trained it on the air behind her. This time it was set to maximum.

The glacial crashed into her and Adria slammed backwards into the snow. Miraculously, she was still holding the pistol. The glacial had landed on top of her. The hideous blue creature was already hunkering down against her legs, lapping up the few degrees of heat that were coming away from the suit. She pointed and fired, searing a perfect hollow down the length of the monster, straight through the cheek and out of its back.

The glacial screamed and leapt off her. And no wonder. It was red hot in places, and on fire.

The snowmen loved heat, but superheat anything and it's going to have a really bad day. Thermite pistols were powerful enough to split water molecules and burn the resulting hydrogen. She hadn't melted it; she'd ignited it.

Adria winced as she pulled herself up. Her legs were so cold they ached and she had no way to rub warmth back into them.

'You're okay,' she assured herself through ragged breaths. 'You're okay.'

The glacial was moaning into the snow, trying to cool down again, but she knew what would happen.

'One less snowman,' she sighed.

She turned back to the bandstand and gasped.

'No......'

There were more of them, dozens, lurching towards her like zombies. Some of them might have been men, once, but others had three legs and moved like tripods. Others could have been arachnids. Most were slow, but some came quickly, like the first.

The same disaster that brought the gravitons raining down on Earth had also brought the cold, and the glacials. No one understood why, any more than they understood the human soul.

Adria would have a few minutes to ponder it herself as they swarmed her and sucked the warmth out of her body until she died of hypothermia.

Adria let the suit's weight pull her to her knees. She raised her right arm and aimed the pistol. A few more good thermite shots would at least make her feel like she'd put up a fight.

Adria had almost squeezed the trigger when she realised – the snowmen *weren't* coming towards her. They were homing in on their dying friend instead! He was the greater source of heat now. The burning hydrogen was giving off enough energy to pull in every glacial nearby. Adria wasn't even a blip on their radar.

She tried to stand again.

No! Her legs might as well have been frozen already. She pushed upwards as hard as she could, trying to lift her weight off the ground. Nothing was happening. The suit didn't even have the power to lift itself anymore. If Adria pulled with all her might she was strong enough to lift her arms, but that was all.

She could always exit the suit, but the cold would kill her almost instantly.

Would that be better, though? To die now, on her terms, rather than wait until the glacials decided she was worth sucking dry? It'd be faster.

Adria gritted her teeth and lifted her hands to her helmet. Three clips: one primary and two redundant. She was breathing even harder now than when she was running. A tear was tickling her cheek. She couldn't see the hydrogen flames from the snowman she had shot anymore. One of the glacials had already lost interest and was moving towards her. She had to do it now.

Adria undid the first clip. She braced her fingers against the second and pressed.

Something grabbed her hand.

The Captain's grizzled face was staring down at her. He was breathing hard, and his visor was steaming up with each exhalation. His eyes were locked on hers and he was shouting orders, even though he must have known she couldn't hear him.

Suddenly he wrapped her in a bear hug and he mouthed something to her. It looked like... *hold on*?

She gripped his suit as hard as she could.

A moment later they were both lurched off their feet. The Captain's tether had gone taut and they were shooting across the ground like a bobsleigh, casting a wave of snow on either side. They smashed through two glacials which burst into shards of ice.

The Captain had one arm wrapped around the tether and was holding onto her suit with both hands. They clanged against the bandstand and kept going, lifting up, up into the sky.

With the last of her suit's power Adria reached down to her left leg and patted the graviton source in her pocket.

Mission accomplished.

Robin Friday
Steve Partridge

Today's top professional footballers have both team and personalised fitness and training schedules which include special diets based on chicken, pasta, vegetables and rest. There is a strong emphasis on discipline, focusing on the specific job a player is given within the system played by the team; there are fewer opportunities for individuals to fully express themselves. Compare the lifestyle and play of today's professionals to those of Robin Friday, a legendary centre forward who played for Reading in the 1970s.

On 27th January 1974, the then Reading FC manager Charlie Hurley signed a 22-year-old centre forward Robin Friday from non-league Hayes. As a young player, he had been rejected by Crystal Palace, Queens Park Rangers and Chelsea because of his non-conformist style of play. He had also served a 16-month sentence in Borstal for persistent misdemeanours such as theft and robbery. His father had said of him, 'He just doesn't care.'

Robin Friday made his living as an asphalter. It was rumoured he could lay a tarmac drive on a Saturday morning, lay a lady at lunchtime, score a sensational goal for Reading in the afternoon, then drink, dance and take drugs for the remainder of the weekend. He would turn up for training sometime on Tuesday or Wednesday. In two spells with Hayes he scored 46 goals in 67 appearances, a remarkable achievement. His positive attributes were his physical strength, his will to win, his football intelligence, his ball skills and his ability to score and make goals for other players.

Jimmy Andrews, his former manager at Cardiff City, the club he joined after leaving Reading in 1976, said, 'He was the complete centre forward.'

Friday signed as professional for Reading on 6th February 1974, ten days after he had made his first team debut as an amateur against Northampton Town. The *Evening Post* described his performance in a 3-3 draw as 'outstanding.' After scoring in the 2-1 defeat at Barnsley on 10th February, on his professional debut, Friday scored twice when Reading defeated Exeter City 4-1. This time the *Evening Post* said his performance was 'sheer magic', and his first goal, when he ran down the left wing, beat four Exeter players and shot into the opposite side of the goal, was reported as 'glorious'. Friday's hair rested on the top of his shoulders. He played with his shirt outside of his shorts, which finished just above his knees. He didn't wear shin guards and his socks were slumped around his ankles. He was, to say the least, individualistic, if not downright attention-seeking. He was, of course, an immediate hit with the Elm Park faithful because, after his introduction into the team, Reading scored sixteen goals in five games.

While his performances on the pitch were attracting the attention of scouts from top clubs, his behaviour in the pubs and clubs of Reading was attracting the attention of the police. He was banned from Caversham's Crown public house for dancing on the tables and barred 10 times from the Boar's Head in the town. In Churchill's nightclub he danced naked except for a pair of hobnail boots and was regularly barred from the Sindlesham Mill nightclub for doing a dance called the elephant which involved pulling out the pockets of his jeans and exposing himself. He drank excessively wherever he socialised and was never less than boisterous.

At the start of the 1974-75 season, he came back late to Elm Park from a prolonged holiday in a hippie commune in Cornwall. Despite his lack of fitness, after scoring his first hat trick for the club against Southport by 30th September he was the Football League's joint top goal scorer. But there were more problems on and off the field. He had his name taken by referees on three occasions and the *Evening Post* was critical of his 'completely unnecessary and stupid infractions.' His antics included squeezing opposing players' testicles in an attempt to break their concentration, and on one away trip he walked drunk into the bar of the hotel where the team were staying carrying a swan. By the end of the season Reading had finished in seventh place, Friday had scored 20 goals and was voted player of the year.

The 1975-76 season was to be his best and last full season for Reading. The club gained promotion, he scored 22 goals and was again voted player of the season. He got married for the second time. The wedding was filmed by Southern Television, where Friday was seen dressed in a brown velvet suit rolling a joint. The 200 guests, mostly from London, got very drunk, started fighting each other and stealing the wedding presents, which included a large quantity of cannabis. Friday's bride Liza Deimel, a Reading-born university graduate said the wedding was 'the most hilarious thing ever.'

The highlight of the season for Robin Friday was a goal he scored against Tranmere Rovers. From a high pass he jumped up, and with his back to the goal, controlled the ball on his chest, turned and volleyed it over his shoulder into the net 25 yards away. The ball rocketed into top right-hand corner of the goal, stunning the crowd into silence. International referee Clive Thomas said, 'Even up against the likes of Pele and Cruyff, that is the best goal I have ever seen.'

Friday replied, 'You should come here more often, ref. I do that every week.'

In October 1977, Robin Friday transferred to Cardiff City after his behaviour became too much for the then Reading manager Charlie Hurley. He only played 21 games for the Bluebirds, scoring six goals, but in that time he became as much a legend with them as he had been with Reading. In 1999, he won the title 'Player of the Millennium' from Reading and was voted 'All-time Cult Hero' for both Reading and Cardiff City in a 2004 BBC poll.

He died, aged 38, on 22nd December 1990 in Acton of a suspected heroin overdose. Hundreds of people attended the funeral. In 1996, the Cardiff-based band Super Furry Animals issued a single with a cover showing Robin Friday playing for Cardiff City at Ninian Park. They dedicated it to his memory. The title of the song was *The Man Don't Give a Fuck*.

Boys Never Grow Up
Steve Partridge

We breeze in through Caversham and take the Henley Road down to the crem in All Hallows road. The twin Dolomite engines in my white 1969 Triumph Stag bubbling and burbling away like a saucepan of potatoes on the hob. It's a warm April afternoon and I've got the hood down so we can enjoy the sunshine. We chug, unnoticed as always, into the nearest car park, jump out and then walk slowly towards the crem to see if anybody we know has arrived before us.

My all-time great mate Parns, Alan Parnell, doesn't go to funerals to pay his respects to the deceased, he goes to talk about the living. His thoughts are never for the departed, they are always for the attending mourners. 'Do you remember Brenda Gosling? Worked in accounts at Courages. She popped my cherry for me when I was 16. And look at Geoff McGuire in his Bentley. He must have a rich wife, or he's won the lottery. He can't have paid for that himself. He was a thicko at school.'

And so he rabbits on at every funeral we go to; he never pays much attention to the service. For him it's just a game of spot the mourner, a nostalgia trip back to the sixties and seventies when we were carefree young men living life for a laugh.

Parns and I have been friends since we were five. We were always energetic, into everything, climbing trees, falling out of them, coming off our bikes. Both of us were close to fearless. The type of boys psychiatrists worry about. We went through school together, played in the same football teams, and the same band, The Hexham Blues Brothers. Got drunk together, if there was ruck in the pub we were up for it, we were inseparable. They called us the terrible twins. We even shared our girlfriends. That caused some problems for a while, but we stuck together, we wouldn't let anything come between us. We bought motorbikes and cars at the same time, rode and drove like lunatics; our parents and later on our wives, never went to sleep at night until they heard the front door close and knew we were home safe, which was nearly always.

For the past 20 years we've been going to funerals together. Just one every two or three years to start with but in recent times as people have got older it has increased to three or four a year. Parns reads the obituary column in the Chronicle every week, calls me if he spots someone we know. He doesn't own a car anymore, I was with him when he had an accident a while back, it finished him with driving. Finished both of us for most things. So I have to pick him up and drive us to the church or the crem. On a couple of occasions he has been so preoccupied with searching for familiar faces in the congregation he's forgotten who we've come to say goodbye to.

'Poor old Harry.'

'Harry was last time, Parns. It's Hoppy today.'

'What? So it is. Sorry, Hoppy. How could I forget it was Hoppy? He sang and played harmonica in the band with us. One day we'll be the only two left from the old days. What will we do then?'

Outside the crem he gives me a run down on the mourners. He rattles off verbal pen pictures of nearly everyone in the queue for the chapel. Details going back to their teenage days, escapades and things they got up to, a résumé of lovers, wives, husbands and exes. Their children inside and outside of wedlock, affairs, one night stands, embarrassing anecdotes, convictions and gaol sentences, cars they've owned, even down to model numbers and registration plates. He has a memory like a herd of elephants. It's all stored away on his cerebral hard drive and available for immediate broadcast on Radio Parns. Repeats available on Parns Player by request.

We follow the coffin into the crem. Fairport Convention are playing *Who Knows Where The Time Goes*. Sandy Denny's poignant voice is licking off the walls like slow motion waves rolling in with the tide.

Family on the left, friends on the right. Seven of us, including Parns, all sat together for the first time in years; the remnants of the Hexham Road FC team that won the double in '73. We all came from the Hexham Road estate in Reading; grew up there in the sixties. We used to say, 'Hexham Road through the middle of us, like a stick of rock.' We are eight rows down on the right hand side. Sitting behind us are some old friends from the estate and Hoppy's colleagues from Reading General Hospital where he worked as a porter. Directly in front of us, two rows down, there's a guy with a broad back and big shoulders sat on his own.

Hoppy was our 'keeper, huge, built like a slab of granite, nerveless, a big occasion player; he would have made it as a pro with Reading but for his stutter. Parns and I were the centre backs; when the crosses, corners and free kicks came in we'd call it for him, 'Hoppy's ball.' He'd come flying off his line, spring off his left foot, right foot raised up high, hands like shovels, clamping onto the ball.

He would shout. 'G-G-Got it!'

No problem. No one messed with Hoppy.

He saved a penalty in the last minute of the cup final against Maidenhead Social Club. Social's centre forward followed up and kicked him in the head. We went mad. Chased the toe-rag off the pitch. He locked himself in the dressing room. After the game Hoppy just laughed. 'I-I t-t-thought th-hat kick in the head m-m-might fix this. B-butt it b-bleeding didn't. I'll f-fix him next s-season.'

We all laughed, tipped the contents of the cup over his head, picked him up and threw him into the bath with his kit on.

Some sanguine words from the priest, prayers, and an emotional tribute from his eldest son. He told the congregation what a great father Hoppy was, took care of him when his mum died, coached him to be a 'keeper, encouraged him to get a degree, told him not to put up with any nonsense from anybody. One of the best.

More prayers, followed by *Abide With Me*. Instinctively on the last note the seven of us leap up together, hands in the air above our heads, we shout, 'Hoppy's ball.' As we call it, the guy with the big shoulders two rows in front of us jumps up and turns around all in one movement. His huge hands clamped onto a football in front of his face.

'G-G-Got it!' he says.

We are both mesmerized. As stiff as a pair of starched sheets on a washing line, staring directly at him.

He drops his hands down to the centre of his chest and

pulls the ball into his body. We're speechless. I look at Parns, he's still transfixed. But I can see the wheels turning in his head as he commits to memory what he is witnessing. He wants to get this story right for the next funeral we go to, that's for sure.

Hoppy looks at Parns and throws the ball to him. Parns catches it, pulls it into his body, just like Hoppy. Still shocked, Parns returns Hoppy's look. Without moving his eyes he passes me the ball. The music changes to *Goodbye Blues* by The Hexham Blues Brothers. When Hoppy walks out from his seat and down the aisle towards the curtains which are beginning to close behind his coffin he is listening to himself sing and blow the harp. We follow him and head for the curtains as well, all three of us must go through them before they close. Just like Parns and I have done for the past 20 years at every funeral we've been to, including the first one, when we were in the coffins and the congregation. Just like Hoppy is today.

20 years back Parns was gunning his E-Type along the A339 to Basingstoke when he had a blow-out. I was sat in the passenger seat next to him. A couple of middle-aged, devil-may-care boy racers who finally ran out of luck, just opposite the Duke of Wellington's statue.

ALSO BY READING WRITERS
www.readingwriters.co.uk

Set out on a journey in Reading Writers' 2014 anthology, *Voyages*. Choose any path you wish. Join heroes and heroines of all kinds; frantic criminals, fairytale creatures, Arapaho Indians, cowboys, refugees, lovers, murderers and aliens on marvellous adventures in worlds both strange and familiar. Visit cities and countryside, travel through Britain and Europe, America and Asia, and press on, out into space and on to the deepest realms of fantasy. Face love, loss and grief, take on assassins, tread new ground and embrace the thrill of romance. It's all here.

Reading Writers' 2011 anthology, *Another Light Raid*, contains poetry, fiction and non-fiction by 16 local authors and is available both as a print book and an eBook.

'This anthology contains some of the best writing going on in Reading…' says award-winning thriller writer Patrick Lennon in his introduction.